American Mathematical Society
P. O. Box 6248, Providence, Rhode Island 02940
Telephone (401) 272-9500

I HAVE A PHOTOGRAPHIC MEMORY

PAUL R. HALMOS

ERRATA

Due to an error, photographs #496 and #502
were interchanged. We apologize for any
inconvenience this may cause.

Location: 201 Charles Street at Randall Square

I Have A Photographic Memory

PAUL R. HALMOS

I Have
A Photographic Memory

— 1987 —

AMERICAN MATHEMATICAL SOCIETY

PROVIDENCE, RHODE ISLAND

Library of Congress Cataloging-in-Publication Data

Halmos, Paul R. (Paul Richard), 1916–

    I have a photographic memory.

    Includes index.
    1. Mathematicians–Portraits. 2. Mathematics–
History–Pictorial works. I. Title.
QA28.H345 1987   510′.92′2   87-33450
ISBN 0-8218-0115-5 (alk. paper)

Preface

Would you look at some of the snapshots I have taken in the last 40-odd years?

If you put a penny into a piggy bank every day for 45 years, you'll end up with something over 16,000 pennies. I have been a snapshot addict for more than 45 years, and I have averaged one snapshot a day. Over a third of the pictures so accumulated have to do with the mathematical world: they are pictures of mathematicians, their spouses, their brothers and sisters and other relatives, their offices, their dogs, and their carillon towers. The pictures were taken at the universities where I worked, and the places where I was a visitor (for a day or for a year), and, as you will see, many of them were taken over food and drink. That's rather natural, if you think about it. It is not easy, and often just not possible, to snap mathematicians at work (in a professional conversation, thinking, lecturing, reading)—it is much easier to catch them at tea or at dinner or in a bar. In any event, the result of my hobby was a collection of approximately 6000 "mathematical" pictures, and when it occurred to me to share them with the world I faced an extremely difficult problem of choice.

The amounts of available space and available money (in the publishing world the words are almost synonymous) led quickly to the conclusion that I could publish only about 10 per cent of what I had; how was that 10 per cent to be chosen? My answer turned out to be sometimes random, and usually more personal than professional. The people included are not necessarily the greatest mathematicians or the best known. If I think a picture is striking, or interesting, or informative, or nostalgic, then it is here, even if the theorems its subject has proved are of less mathematical depth than those of a colleague whose office is two doors down the hall. If your favorite mathematician is not here, please forgive me, and if your picture is not flattering, blame yourself and me in equal proportion.

Decisions had to be made other than just in or out. What was I to do when I had two pictures of the same person? Sometimes I included both (if, for instance, someone is just marginally and unrecognizably part of a picture, or if I felt like doing so for some other reason), but when I made a choice I chose the one in which the subject was younger. That seemed to me to have greater personal and perhaps even greater historical interest.

I am a snapshot shooter, not a photographer. The pictures in this book are not art; their only possible significance comes from your interest in whom they show. Even as snapshots, the quality of the pictures is highly variable. Some are acceptable—clear and sharp—and others are fuzzy, out of focus, barely recognizable. I am sorry about the latter kind, but that's how they came out, and if the subject is of sufficient interest I decided to include the picture anyway.

The captions that accompany the pictures vary from a part of a line to a long paragraph. You have probably encountered the name of most subjects here represented (as an author, as a colloquium speaker, as a teacher, or as the subject of an interesting bit of professional gossip) and are curious to see the face it

Preface

belongs to. Possibly you have seen the person and are pleased to have a reminder on your bookshelf. In either case, you need no further identification than a hint at affiliation, specialization, or family connection. On a few occasions captions serve to avoid confusion—is this Conway the group theorist or the functional analyst? In such cases I tried to include a bit more information than would be strictly necessary. If I happen to know a small anecdote, a bit of not universally known history, the caption becomes longer. If, on the other hand, the caption is nearly vanishing, the reason is either that I think no more is needed or, more often, that no more is known to me. In such cases I ask you to forgive my ignorance, and I ask that you not interpret brevity as a put-down. You will notice perhaps that the captions get more chatty as the years go on—I remember more about the recent pictures, and, in case I have forgotten something, it is easier to get the missing information.

The more recent pictures are the ones nearer the end: the order is more or less chronological. The rule of thumb (put earlier pictures near the beginning) is deliberately violated on some occasions. When a caption of one picture mentions a relative or a colleague or a collaborator whose picture was taken years later, I have often decided to re-unite a pair of friends or relatives whom the accident of being seen by me at different times has artificially separated. Warning: this quasi-rational violation of chronology is itself violated sometimes. Thus, for instance, Hodge and Pedoe are neighbors in this book, even though their pictures were taken four years apart, but Felix Browder and Bill Browder, whose pictures were taken a dozen years apart, remain apart. Such things are of concern to authors and editors, but all that a reader needs to know is the general principle (ordered by time) and the possible existence of counterexamples (if you don't find someone you are looking for next to a close personal or professional relative, keep looking).

The naming system is one I learned from the AMS many years ago (but I am not sure whether the AMS still follows it): if a person has two or more names in addition to a family name, they are represented by initials (as in D. G. Higman), but if the entire name has only two parts, then both are spelled out (as in Graham Higman). The index, however, lists initials only, no matter how few or how many of them there are.

One final word, which makes contact with the delicate problem of whose picture appears in this book. One necessary condition for a picture to be here is that I myself took it, and even that rule has two exceptions. This book was not designed to be and is not a book of photographs of myself, but it does contain two pictures of me. In one of those (#455) I am almost not there at all, and certainly not recognizable, but I happen to be an essential part of the picture. In the other (#581) I am there all right, and so are three other people, and I didn't have the heart to cut myself out. Please forgive me for these exceptions.

I hope you like the book. I do. It has faults that I am more aware of than most readers, but I think collections like this can be interesting, and, who knows?, perhaps valuable. Have fun.

P.R.H.

Contents

I Have A Photographic Memory

Chicago and vicinity, the early 50's

1 – 38

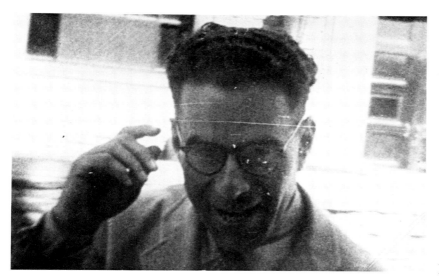

Witold Hurewicz

A topologist of lasting renown, he is the father of higher-dimensional homotopy, but he is perhaps best known to non-specialists for his book on dimension theory (with Henry Wallman). Sometimes he seemed to live in a universe slightly different from that of the rest of us—he was absent-minded and bewildered by the details of daily life. He could and did drive a car, but his speed was a function of his concentration on the mathematics under discussion—fast when things were going well and a crawl when he was stuck. There were many stories about his woolliness, a lot of them probably made up. For instance: he drove to New York one time (from Cambridge), forgot that he did so, took the train home, and next morning, not finding his car parked in front of his house, reported that the car had been stolen. For all I know it's true. He died in a mountaineering accident in Mexico—he was alone, put his foot in the wrong place, slipped, and fell. The picture was taken in 1942.

Harish-Chandra

Harish (who denied having a "first name" in the usual American sense) was a born physicist, but he saw the light and became an inspired and admired member of the highly abstract mathematical community. He complained once to Dirac, whose assistant he was at the time, that although he had discovered what he believed was the answer to the question they had been asking, he was not able to find the proof. "I don't care about proofs" Dirac told him; "I want to know the truth." The picture was taken at the 1950 Summer meeting of the AMS in Boulder.

3

Nándor Balázs and P. A. M. Dirac
Speaking of Dirac, here he is, in Cambridge (England, that is) in 1968, with Balázs (left), a Hungarian physicist, currently at Stony Brook.

Beno Eckmann
An algebraic topologist, for a long time on the faculty of the ETH (Eidgenössische Technische Hochschule) in Zürich, and the main editor of the "yellow peril" Grundlehren series. This is what he looked like in August 1951 (in Chicago).

4

L. A. Santaló

One of the leading lights of the small mathematical community of Argentina, his name was for a long time synonymous with his specialty, integral geometry. Here he is in Punta del Este, Uruguay, in 1951.

5

6

S. L. Warner

The main feature of functional analysis in its early days seemed to be that it bestowed a topology on algebraic structures (for example, vector spaces). Some people thought that "topological algebra" was the right name for a subject that did that, but the name didn't stick. Topological algebra, however, and, in particular, topological groups, topological rings, and topological fields, is just what Seth Warner has been studying. The picture was taken in 1951.

L. E. J. Brouwer

Some people try hard to be remembered for one great contribution; Brouwer will be remembered for two. He discovered deep theorems in topology (remember fixed points) and he created intuitionism. When I saw him (at the Kingston meeting of the AMS in 1953) he had the un-self-conscious zeal of a missionary, which allowed him, for instance, to take a little over two hours to deliver a one-hour invited address.

8

Maurice Auslander and R. W. Barnard

The 1950s was one of the great periods of the University of Chicago. On the third floor of Eckhart Hall you were likely to bump into the then famous mathematicians (some of whom are no longer remembered very clearly) and the youngsters at the beginnings of their careers (who have become famous since then). Ray Barnard (right) was one of the last survivors of the E. H. Moore tradition of general analysis; Maurice Auslander was just beginning to climb the (algebraic) ladder of groups and rings and modules and things.

9

Bernice Auslander

Bunny is not only a mathematician but also a mathematician's (Maurice's) wife.

10

Louis Auslander

Lou is not only a mathematician but also a mathematician's (Maurice's) brother. His picture belongs here, with his relatives, even though theirs were taken in the 1950s and his not till 1978, when he came to give a colloquium talk in Bloomington. He works on solvmanifolds and flows and Lie groups.

G. E. Backus, Joseph Bram, and R. J. Nunke

Here are some of the most promising beginners at Chicago in the 1950s: Ronald Nunke (left), Joe Bram, one of my best Ph.D. students (center), and George Backus.

12

J. J. Rotman

Another bright Chicagoan, Joe came along slightly later; this picture was taken in 1959. He became an abelian groupie with excursions to homology.

Morris Schreiber and Jerome Spanier

Two others who made teaching at Chicago a pleasure in the 1950s: Moe on the left (I was proud to have him as a Ph.D. student) and Jerry (who grew up to be Vice President for Academic Affairs and Dean of the Faculty at Claremont Graduate School).

13

14

L. V. Hörmander and E. H. Spanier

Speaking of Spaniers, here is Jerry's older brother Ed (right) with Lars Hörmander, on the river Clyde during an excursion from the 1958 Edinburgh Congress. Ed is best known for his topological contributions, including his standard-setting text, and Lars, a disciple of Marcel Riesz, is a leading partial differential equator.

15

Alexander Grothendieck

Grothendieck was a visitor at Chicago when this picture was taken. At that time he had hair and he was a spectacularly prolific contributor to functional analysis; since then he is usually seen with his head shaved, and he is usually known as an algebraic geometer and a fiery political activist.

16

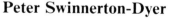

Peter Swinnerton-Dyer

In the 1950s he was just a young visitor at Chicago, with as English an English accent as you've ever heard, who came to be near André Weil. Since then he has become Sir Peter, a number theorist famous for both his work and his challenging conjectures, and he has been Master of St. Catharine's College and Vice Chancellor of Cambridge University.

W. H. Cockcroft

A topologist and a friendly beer drinker (in the 1950s in Chicago), Bill has spent a lot of his time and energy on mathematical administration, including a period as Vice Chancellor at the New University of Ulster, in Northern Ireland. Having been knighted for his services, he should now be called Sir Wilfred, but I refuse. Several mathematicians whom I knew when they were young, and not yet important, became knighted since then, but, I was told, the reason is always public service of some kind—never mathematics.

17

18

Armand Borel, Shiing-Shen Chern, R. K. Lashof, and André Weil

Each of this group was a Chicago faculty member when the picture was taken (in 1955). Reading from left to right, they are: Borel, the back of Weil's head, Chern, and Lashof. As for Borel, this one is no relation to the other one; Armand is Swiss and Émile was French. Borel and Weil went to the Institute, and Chern and Lashof ended up in Berkeley. Lashof was the last to leave, and in half a sense he hasn't left yet; he told me that he was spending one term each year at Chicago (which means about three or four months out of twelve).

19

Reinhold Baer and Erwin Kleinfeld

Reinhold (left) was a leading group theorist—
he helped many young people into mathematical
research and then watched them become leaders
themselves. He was never on the permanent
faculty at Chicago, but he was a frequent visitor.
Erwin was a member of the faculty when this
picture was taken (in the Common Room on the
second floor of Eckhart Hall).

20

J. F. Nash and J. W. T. Youngs

John (right) is a non-cooperative game theorist
(a non-associative phrase) who has also written
about cooperative games, and is famous for his
imbedding theorem for Riemannian manifolds.
Ted (the last of the three initials is the one
that counts) worked on the topology and the
area theory of surfaces, but his most memorable
contribution was his joint work with Ringel (#596)
on the settling of the Heawood conjecture about
the coloring of maps for surfaces of every genus
other than 0.

21

L. J. Savage

A differential geometer who became a leading statistician, and whom only direct mail advertisers ever addressed as Leonard; his name was Jimmie (not James or Jim). Among his major contributions are the books *The foundations of statistics* and (with Lester Dubins, #427) *How to gamble if you must.*

22

I. R. Savage

Richard is Jimmie's brother and a well-known statistician in his own right; he has been at Yale for a long time. This picture was taken in Ann Arbor in 1967.

23

L. M. Graves and O. F. G. Schilling

Lawrence (left) was a gentleman of the old school and a mathematician of what by now has become the old school; his interest was in the kind of real variable theory that was modern and radical in the 1920s. His text was widely used for a while. Otto was an algebraist who collaborated on several papers with Saunders Mac Lane (#24). Both Lawrence and Otto were very much part of the 1950s scene at Chicago, but they were considered members of the old guard whom the "Young Turks" were displacing.

H. L. Hamburger and Saunders Mac Lane

Hans Hamburger (right) bears the name of the famous moment problem. He was a heavy smoker and a confirmed night person; when he lived in Ankara he became well known at the all night café where he did all his work. The name of Saunders, a reformed smoker, is associated with category theory; he has served as president of both the MAA and the AMS.

24

25

W. A. Ambrose and Ernst Straus

The next six or eight pictures, including this one, belong to the same period as the ones before it, but not to the same place. They were taken here and there, at professional meetings, or, sometimes, just on the occasion of private visits. Ann Arbor, in particular, was very much on my visiting list, and that's where Ambrose (only his mother and his wife call him Warren) and Ernst (left) were snapped. Ambrose worked on stochastic processes, ergodic theory, and then differential geometry and partial differential equations. Straus, like several others in this collection, was a reformed physicist, one time assistant to Einstein, and a superbly informed and intelligent mathematician who could be especially helpful if you were stuck on something in combinatorics or number theory.

S. S. Cairns

Stewart was a topologist and then an administrator; he was chairman of the mathematics departments at Syracuse and then at Illinois.

26

27

Herman Chernoff and H. J. Greenberg

Herman (left) is in statistics, and he has been associated with Stanford, then with MIT, and, most recently, with Harvard. Herbie is an applied type; for a while he was chairman at the University of Denver.

Allen Devinatz and John Wermer

Analysts both, Allen (right) at Northwestern and John at Brown. Allen knows more about positive definite functions than anyone should; John has worked in operator theory and, mostly, in several complex variables.

28

T. H. Hildebrandt

Nobody of my generation ever dared to call him Ted. He was chairman at Michigan for a long time and a power in the American mathematical community. Although he acted vague and fuzzy, and giggled and scratched his head nervously when he made one of his frequent malapropisms, most of us considered him someone to be scared of. Mathematically he was a pioneer in abstract integration theory and in Banach spaces.

30

Nathan Jacobson and C. E. Rickart

Jake (left) is one of the major American figures in algebra, with many contributions to, for instance, the theory of non-associative algebras, and many famous texts; he took his Ph.D. in Princeton, in 1934, under the supervision of the legendary Wedderburn. Chuck (Charlie to some) is a powerful analyst known for his work on Banach algebras (his book was for a long time the standard source of information about the subject) and several complex variables. Here they are in the celebrated Pretzel Bell in Ann Arbor.

Isaac Namioka

When this picture was taken (about 1955) Isaac was not famous yet; the book, with Kelley, on topological vector spaces didn't come out till 1961. (The book has the names of eight other people on the title page, but, apparently, only Kelley and Namioka are properly called its authors.)

31

D. C. Spencer

Don worked (collaborating quite a bit with Kunihiko Kodaira) on frighteningly difficult mathematics (deformations of complex manifolds). He not only worked on them—he saw them; he is a born geometer.

32

33

L. A. Henkin

This picture is the first of a small batch taken during a visit to Berkeley in 1956. Leon is a logician who since then has become more and more interested in matters of education; he has also served as chairman of the mathematics department at Berkeley more than once.

34

35

David Blackwell

David is both a pure mathematician, who knows about some of the fanciest parts of what is known as descriptive set theory, and a statistician, who can use fancy set theory to get results that other statisticians regard as important.

J. W. Green

Johnny had a beard when I snapped him in Berkeley, in 1956, but he didn't always have one—it would come and go. He served as Secretary of the AMS for nine years—a long time, but considerably under the average.

36

G. P. and R. H. Hochschild

I have been cutting my own hair, with clippers, for a long time; inspired thereby, Ruth Hochschild decided to try them on Gerhard. The Hochschild cohomology groups of algebras were already in existence when this picture was taken in 1956.

David Lowdenslager

David (here shown in Berkeley, in 1956) was an excellent sailor, as well as a functional analyst and, in particular, operator theorist; it's a pity he died young.

John Myhill

John was a colorful character, an excited but not always crystal clear lecturer. His forte was to axiomatize everything. Bishop didn't think that his (Bishop's) intuitionist-like constructivism could or should be axiomatized, but the last I heard he grudgingly came around and agreed that Myhill's way of doing it was acceptable. While axiomatizing recalcitrant subjects, John learned a lot about a lot of mathematics, but he continued to occupy himself mainly with set theory. One of his earliest accomplishments was to prove that, despite the existence of uncountably many sets but only countably many names, the hypothesis that every set is nameable is consistent with customary axiomatic set theory.

The Edinburgh Congress,
1958

39 – 69

H. P. Cartan and Jean-Pierre Serre

The 1958 Congress in Edinburgh was one of my most fruitful sources of mathematical photographs; this picture was taken there and so were its successors, till further notice. Henri Cartan (left) has studied analytic functions in various numbers of variables, and he has studied sheaves, and homological algebra, and potential theory; and he is, incidentally, the son of another great mathematician, Élie Cartan. Serre got the Fields medal in 1954 for finding out more than his predecessors about the homotopy groups of spheres, but that didn't make him stop doing mathematics; he has contributed to our knowledge of algebraic geometry, and Lie groups and Lie algebras.

39

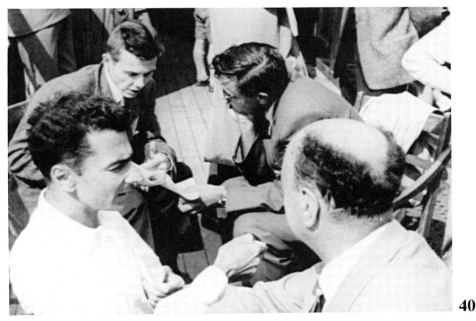

40

Richard Brauer, Serge Lang, I. R. Shafarevich, and J. T. Tate

Organized excursions are not always the best parts of Congresses, but the boat trip on the Clyde was a successful social event. The four socializers in this picture, clockwise from the left, are Serge Lang (already an active algebraist, but not yet known as the anti-bureaucratic conscience of the mathematical world), John Tate (who is, incidentally, Artin's son-in-law), Shafarevich, and, represented by the back of his head, Richard Brauer.

41

Börge Jessen

A great Dane to know and a super analyst (measures and integrals), another socializer on the river Clyde.

42

P. S. Alexandroff and Yu. M. Smirnov

Alexandroff-Hopf used to be the way to pronounce *Topologie*, and here on the right is that Alexandroff. (There are too many ways of transliterating even relatively simple Russian names such as this one; the version I am using is the one that appears in the book.) Smirnov was near the beginning of his career at the Edinburgh Congress; all I remember is that he spoke about infinite-dimensional spaces.

A. D. Alexandroff

Speaking of Alexandroffs, here is the other one, the measure theorist in Siberia.

A. G. Kurosh

The group theorist. When I met him (on the river Clyde, in 1958), he had never seen a Polaroid picture, and he spoke no English, but he was so excited and happy at getting an instant copy of himself that he had no trouble expressing his gratitude.

44

45

S. L. Sobolev

A discoverer and developer of generalized functions (distributions) and $W^{m,p}$ spaces.

46

I. M. James

Not everyone on the Clyde excursion was from the Soviet Union; here is one counterexample. Ioan is a fine British topologist; the spelling of his first name, however, is something I always have to look up before I need it.

47

Helmut Kneser

One of a family of mathematical Knesers whom it is sometimes hard to tell apart; this one is interested in what might be called the analysis of algebra, the properties of the solutions of polynomial and power series equations.

W. W. Rogosinski

Before harmonic analysis came
to mean the theory of the char-
acters of locally compact abelian
groups it used to mean the study
of the pointwise convergence
properties of Fourier series, and
that's what Rogosinski is known
for.

George Pólya

Most famous for his classical problem book (known as Pólya-Szegö), he is also revered as the godfather of combinatorics.

49

50

L. J. Mordell and Gábor Szegö

Speaking of Szegö, here he is (right). Mordell was a great number theorist, known for, among other things, the deep conjecture (related to Fermat's last "theorem") that was proved by Faltings (#579) in 1983.

Kosaku Yosida
Leading Japanese functional analyst, occasional collaborator of Kakutani, as he appeared in Edinburgh in 1958.

51

Hans Freudenthal
A Dutch homotopist and topological groupie, and, incidentally, one of the few mathematicians actively interested in making contact with extraterrestrial intelligence.

52

53

Helmut Wielandt

A group theorist, who published a book on "practical" matrix theory, and who is also known to operator theorists for being one of the first to prove that the identity in a Banach algebra cannot be a commutator.

Andrzej Mostowski

The logical and set-theoretic powerhouse.

54

55

J. H. C. Whitehead

He was known as Henry, and his initials, referring to his lecturing style, were alleged to stand for "Jesus, he's confusing". He was charming and witty with or without a drink. He was a topologist, a nephew of the philosopher Alfred North Whitehead, but not a relative of the American topologist George Whitehead (#509). When George first wrote to Henry, he inquired about the possibility of their being related, and, later, George showed me the answer. As I now remember, it began as follows. "Dear Whitehead: Not that I know of."

C. A. Rogers

Known as Ambrose to his friends, and known to all as one of the discoverers of the Dvoretzky-Rogers theorem, the one about convergence in a Banach space having good properties in the finite-dimensional case only. His greatest interest seems to be in covering and packing problems, which, of course, make contact with measures such as Hausdorff's.

56

57

M. H. Heins and W. V. D. Hodge

Maurice (left) is an analytic functioner who was at Illinois for a long time and then moved to Maryland. Bill Hodge (later Sir William) did algebraic geometry; there is something called a Hodge variety. His book with Pedoe was a large and difficult step forward when it came out.

Daniel Pedoe

Here is Dan Pedoe, Hodge's collaborator, on a visit to Ann Arbor in 1962; I put the picture here, in with the ones taken in Edinburgh, so as to bring Hodge and Pedoe together again.

58

59

M. L. Cartwright

She became Mistress of Girton College (Cambridge), and, later, Dame Mary; here (at the Edinburgh Congress) she is just an outstanding complex analyst. I met her once as she was just arriving from England, and as I was driving her to her hotel I had occasion to refer to someone as a Caspar Milquetoast. The expression can still be found in American dictionaries (referring to a timid cartoon character), but it was not part of her British vocabulary, and I am afraid I bored her when, feeling that I had to, I explained what it meant.

E. C. Zeeman

Chris was just a young topologist trying to find his way in the mathematical world when I first knew him; catastrophe theory, of which he is one of the enthusiastic explainers, came much later.

60

61

Y. N. Dowker, R. G. Swan, G. W. Whitehead, K. B. Whitehead

Although Yael's ergodic theory was of greater personal interest to me than her husband's topology, I met Hugh first (at the Institute). Here she is (right) with George Whitehead (left), Dick Swan peering out from behind George, and Kay Whitehead (who is George's wife, not Henry's).

C. H. Dowker

And, speaking of Hugh Dowker, here he is. He was from Canada originally, but moved to England. He was a persistent but not very good Go player. I didn't get a picture of him at the Edinburgh Congress; this one was taken at the BMC (= British Mathematical Colloquium) in Dundee in 1965.

62

63

Szolem Mandelbrojt

Famous during his lifetime for his work on quasi-analytic functions, nowadays he is remembered also as the uncle of Benoit Mandelbrot (whose last name is spelled differently on purpose). He was a regular visitor to what was then known as the Rice Institute in Texas.

64

Benoit Mandelbrot

Here is Benoit, of fractal fame, at the Laramie meeting of the AMS in 1985, out of chronological order so as to place him next to his uncle.

65

Richard Courant and D. E. Menchoff

Courant (left, foreground) was famous for many things: among them are the analysis book (known as Courant-Hilbert or Hilbert-Courant, depending on your emotions), the calculus book (a standard-setter in the U.S. for several years), and, of course, his leadership of the Courant Institute associated with NYU. Menchoff's work is on the convergence of Fourier series.

A. A. Albert and S. S. Wilks

Adrian (left) was a disciple of the great American number-theorist-algebraist, Leonard Eugene Dickson, and in time he too became one of the foremost algebraists of the U.S. Almost all his professional life was spent at the University of Chicago; he was a patriotic Chicagoan in both the academic and metropolitan senses of the word. He was for a time chairman of the Chicago department and president of the AMS. Sam Wilks was a statistician in the days when the U.S. didn't have many; he was a member of the mathematics department at Princeton.

66

Salomon Bochner

In Princeton he was known as Manya; in the world he was known as one of the greatest experts in Fourier analysis.

67

68

D. H. Lehmer

A number theorist who loves numbers and loves to compute with them, the son of a mathematician and the husband of another.

Emma Lehmer

A collaborator of Dick Lehmer's in more senses than one, she is also a known and respected mathematical translator; we must be grateful to her, in particular, for translating Pontrjagin's *Topological groups*.

69

The Institute and Chicago, the 50's turn to 60's

70 – 100

70

Aryeh Dvoretzky

And here is the Dvoretzky of the Dvoretzky-Rogers theorem, who is usually busy as a probabilist. He is lounging behind the Institute building, in Princeton, in the first of a batch of 1958 pictures that was not taken at the Edinburgh Congress.

C. D. Papakyriakopoulos

Papa, as almost everyone called him, was a shy, modest, gentle person, who loved mathematics (the hard, geometric kind of topology) more than anything else in the world. He didn't always have a job but he kept on going, often working through several nights with just an occasional bit of sleep snatched on a desk top. He didn't resolve the Poincaré conjecture, but his valuable contributions are still remembered and still being used.

71

72

G. T. Whyburn

There were two mathematical Whyburn brothers, G. T. and W. M. This one is Gordon, a topologist, whose interests included the way topology entered into complex function theory. His *Analytic topology* is the only book I know of that is devoted entirely to that connection, but I find it interesting to note that he has another book titled *Topological analysis*. He was president of the AMS for a couple of years and trustee for sixteen (a record?). The picture was taken in September, 1958.

73

F. B. Jones

Burton is a Texas topologist; he sounds like one and he writes like one.

74

B. W. Jones

There was nothing either Texan or topological about this Jones; he was a number theorist who spent most of his professional life at Cornell, but he too was called Burton, and the two Burtons had to solve many problems about misaddressed mail. This Burton moved from Ithaca to Boulder (where this picture was taken in 1963).

75

Lipman Bers

An expert on Teichmüller spaces, a dyed-in-the-wool New Yorker (at Columbia for a long time), and a one-time president of the AMS—all in all a man to be reckoned with. This picture was taken in 1958.

J. V. Wehausen

John was a knowledgeable contributor to the literature of modern analysis and was Executive Editor of Mathematical Reviews for quite a while (1950–1956). That's the real job, not one of the honorary ones. Much of his training and expertise was, however, somewhere else altogether; he is now Professor Emeritus not of mathematics but of naval architecture.

76

77

R. G. Swan

Dick moved to Chicago (which is where this picture was taken in 1958) as a young man, and he stayed. He does algebra of the kind that has to do with algebraic geometry and with homology theory.

78

L. A. Rubel

Lee is an energetic analytic functioner, who looks at the subject from many points of view, including the functionally analytic one. Here he is shown during a Chicago visit. The pictures in the remainder of this chapter were taken during my last two Chicago years (1959–1961) but not necessarily in Chicago.

79

Lars Gårding and Valentine Telegdi

Lars (left) is a partial differential equator of first rank and Val is a physicist, who, despite appearances, is a brilliant conversationalist.

Irving Kaplansky

It's all right to call him Irving, but to most people he is Kap; he even became used to signing letters that way. He got to the top of the heap by being a first-rate doer and expositor of algebra. He was incidentally a remarkably fixed point; despite many invitations to other places, he stayed at Chicago for almost forty years. When retirement approached he moved, and he is now the director of the Mathematical Sciences Research Institute in Berkeley (abbreviated MSRI, pronounced "misery"). That's the place a steep mile and a half up the hill from the University of California whose relations with the university are friendly enough but whose administrative structure is as distant as its geographic location. In his spare time Kap used to play the piano, both classical and jazz, and, when asked, would act as the "rehearsal orchestra" for enthusiasts who were preparing to present a Gilbert and Sullivan opera. He seems also to know all the words to all the popular songs of the first half of this century.

80

Pierre Samuel

Is he a commutative algebraist (see his book with Zariski) or an algebraic geometer?—I am never quite sure I can tell the difference.

81

82

S. B. Kochen and J. R. Shoenfield

Logicians both, at Princeton and at Duke. Si (left) is known for his work (with Ax) on an isomorphism theorem about ultraproducts (which says that a couple of things are the same even if you don't think they should be, and thus settles a conjecture of Artin's about zeros of polynomials over p-adic fields); one among Joe's contributions to the subject is his widely used text on mathematical logic.

Ivan Niven

Ivan is a number theorist, with several highly readable books to his credit; he served a term as president of the MAA.

83

84

E. G. Begle

Ed started out as a topologist, a student of Lefschetz's at Princeton, but then became famous for two other reasons. He was, for one thing, Secretary of the AMS between 1951 and 1956, and, as one of the prime movers of the SMSG (School Mathematics Study Group) he was also one of the prime movers of the "new math". A lot of people liked the SMSG and worked hard for it, but, in the interests of historical honesty, I must report that some others referred to it as Some Mathematics, Some Garbage.

85

A. P. Calderon

Alberto was brought to Chicago by Albert and Stone and Zygmund who were all convinced of his worth, and they were not disappointed; the Calderon-Zygmund work on singular integral operators is just one of the results of the move. On the Chicago faculty for several decades, Alberto always had a part of his heart in Argentina; for a while he was virtually commuting between Buenos Aires and Eckhart Hall.

J. G. Thompson

Finite groups of odd order were not yet solvable when this picture was taken; John's 250 page paper (with Walter Feit), filling an entire issue of the Pacific Journal, came out two years later, in 1963.

86

87

88

J. L. Alperin

Algebra was in good shape at Chicago in 1961 and Jon was, and has continued to be, one of the reasons.

89

J. L. Lions

Another of the glamorous visitors at Chicago, many of whom were invited long before they became internationally famous and glamorous. Jacques Lions' work on interpolation and differential operators in Banach spaces hadn't appeared yet in 1961.

Hugo Steinhaus

He spent the war years in Poland, hiding from the Nazis, going hungry, suffering—and thinking about mathematics. He loved to tell stories of those years. He said, among other things, that the celebrated cake problem (the generalization of "you cut, I choose" to more than two people) was discovered and solved then, not as mathematics for fun but as a genuine difficulty that the persecuted had to face. His mathematical fame is associated with the theory of independent functions (suggested by probability theory), and his expository fame with his beautiful books, including *Mathematical snapshots* and *One hundred problems....* This picture was taken during a visit to Chicago in 1961.

Casimir Kuratowski

A charming and ultra-literate gentleman, Kuratowski was already famous and glamorous in 1960; he was one of the creators of Polish topology. It never would have occurred to me to call him by his first name, but I can't help wondering what it is. Other forms in which it appears in the literature are Kazimir and Kazimierz.

90

91

E. V. Schenkman

Gene was another Chicago visitor, young at the time. He is at Purdue, and he is interested mainly in group theory.

J. L. Kelley

If you make the mistake of writing a good book, your chances of being known and remembered as a mathematician become slimmer than they were before; people tend to forget your papers and remember only that they used your book in a class. Kelley (not to be addressed as either John or Leroy) made that mistake.

Helmut Röhrl

Even if he was one of the solvers of one of Hilbert's problems (Number 21 about the existence of certain differential equations), most people are frightened by the problem of trying to pronounce his name. Can you imagine feeling sorry for someone named Earl and saying "poor Earl"? Just omit the "poo", and you've got it.

J. L. Doob and E. H. Field

Joe became interested in probability before most people were even ready to admit that it is a respectable part of mathematics; as my Ph.D. supervisor (one of my greatest sources of pride) he taught me that it is. His book on stochastic processes is a classic. He came to Illinois in 1935 and, even though he is officially retired now, he is still there. He served as president of both the IMS (Institute of Mathematical Statistics) and the AMS. With him here, in Urbana in 1960, is his wife Elsie, a hard working medical doctor and the mother of three children.

94

95

Joseph Landin and Michio Suzuki

Joe (left) has two qualities that rarely occur together: most people find him easy to get along with and he gets things done. As a result he has been chairman more than once, including a long period at the Chicago campus of the University of Illinois, followed by Ohio State. Suzuki is a group theorist who played a major role in the development of the theory of simple groups. He told me that one of the reasons he didn't accept an attractive offer to move from Illinois to Michigan was that Joe Doob was at Illinois. Doob and Suzuki have no mathematics in common, but Doob's friendship and charisma were worth a lot.

Giovanni Sansone

One of the pleasantest and most effective conferences I ever attended was held in 1960 in the Villa Monastero in the tiny village of Varenna on the Lago di Como. Sansone was "senior officer present"; his mathematical interests were in classical hard analysis, such as ordinary, but usually non-linear, differential equations and orthogonal functions.

96

97

Lawrence Markus

Larry was at Varenna too, but I had known him before in Chicago. His mathematics is control theory.

J. L. Massera

A hard working mathematician (mainly differential equations) and a hard working dedicated political activist (communist member of the parliament in Uruguay); when an extreme rightist government came to power he was arrested, tortured, and kept in jail for eight years. He became "the Massera case", and many mathematicians the world over worked hard and donated funds to try to effect his release. All that happened after this picture (in which he is a member of the Villa Monastero group), and it is all over by now: he is free, living and working in Uruguay.

98

99

C. A. Berger and J. G. Stampfli

The occasion of this picture (taken in 1961) is that I was getting ready to leave Chicago and there seemed to be no way to take my NSF grant to Michigan with me. Albert, Chicago chairman at the time, just hated the idea of not using the remaining funds, so he told me to spend them. "Arrange a conference, or something", he said. A conference was arranged and Charlie (left) and Joe, operator theorists both, were attending it. Charlie doesn't publish much, but he keeps on solving hard problems; the first I remember being impressed by is the so-called power inequality.

K. T. Smith

Kennan is an analyst of many parts, but what I primarily remember him for is the Aronszajn-Smith paper on invariant subspaces for compact operators. Here, in 1961, he accepted my invitation for a last drink, and, as it happened, the last photograph I took as member of the Chicago faculty. The place is the already empty apartment from which we were getting ready to move to Ann Arbor the next day.

100

Mainly Michigan,
the early 60's

101 – 126

101

D. J. Lewis

By going to Ann Arbor I acquired a large number of new colleagues, and among them was my old friend Don Lewis. He was doing number theory then (1961), and has kept doing it ever since, with time out for being chairman of the department for a while.

102

Nathaniel and L. A. Coburn

Nate (left, in the chair) was an applied mathematician, and Lew is his son. A rumor about Nate, which I have not been able to confirm or confute, but which I am passing along as a good story, is that he never assigned a thesis problem to a Ph.D. student unless he himself had already solved it. Then, if the student got stuck and couldn't go on, Nate could and did give powerful help. As for Lew, he later became my "son" in the professional sense, meaning Ph.D. student. He got his degreee in 1964, three years after this picture was taken. For quite a bit of Lew's career he was chairman at Buffalo and apparently a popular and effective chairman too.

D. A. Sánchez

David was a student at Michigan when I first met him (1962); he took topology from me. Last I heard he had become both provost and vice president at Lehigh.

103

104

Wacław Sierpiński

Ann Arbor had its share of glamorous visitors too, and most of us considered Sierpinski to be one of them; the year was 1962. He was one of the major founders of Polish mathematics, a prolific developer of the theory of what have since become known as Polish spaces, and also of cardinal and ordinal number theory. There was a bit of a language problem: he either could not or, in any event, would not speak English, and several of my colleagues and I could not speak French (which was his choice of non-Slavic languages). He lectured in French, and listening to a lecture was easier than trying to make conversation; what with the symbols on the board and catching the occasional word, we ignoramuses could follow most of what was going on.

105

K. W. Gruenberg, J. E. McLaughlin, B. H. Neumann

Jack is at the left, and he was not a glamorous visitor at Michigan but a permanent fixture who quickly became my best friend there. He is an extraordinarily useful algebraist to have around; he knows a lot of non-algebra and is patiently willing to listen to more when you ask him for help. One of the sporadic simple groups bears his name. Karl (middle) and Bernhard are internationally known algebraists too, permanently in London and in Canberra (respectively). Here they are visiting Ann Arbor in 1962.

106

S. A. Gaal

Hungarian by birth (originally Gál), Steve is an analyst by conviction; he is responsible for a fat book called *Linear analysis and representation theory.* Here he is just visiting Ann Arbor.

107

I. L. Gaal

Lisl is not Hungarian by birth, but Czech, and this picture was not taken in Ann Arbor in 1962 but in Vancouver in 1974; there is an obvious reason for putting her picture here anyway. She is a logician, a student of Tarski's, who was Ilse Lisl Novak before she changed her name, and most bibliographies seem to prefer to list her name the way it appears above.

108

H. J. Zassenhaus

Another German algebraist, group theorist in fact, Hans Zassenhaus can certainly be counted among the glamorous Ann Arbor visitors.

109

R. V. Gamkrelidze

Gamkrelidze and Mishchenko were disciples of Pontrjagin in his optimal control period (that seems to be the modern version of the calculus of variations), and they came to Ann Arbor to spend time with Cesari. They spoke English very well, and they became lively members of the mathematical-social life of the town.

110

E. F. Mishchenko

Mishchenko and Gamkrelidze are, obviously, different human beings with almost but not quite identical mathematical interests, but at Michigan they were always together, and that's how they are here.

111

Samuel Eilenberg, G. P. Hochschild, and Alex Rosenberg

Not all the pictures taken during my Michigan days were taken in Michigan; this one, in 1963, is in Berkeley. Alex (left) is an algebraist who was for a long time a loyal and hard-working administrator of the AMS (trustee for ten years). Sammy is Sammy—topologist, homologist, and international operator. His collaborative work with Mac Lane started appearing in 1942. In the early stages they were groping toward the concepts of categories and functors; in 1943 cohomology in abstract groups appears for the first time; and, in 1945, the word "category" sees the light of day. Gerhard (right) has appeared on these pages before (#36).

**Aubert Daigneault and
M. A. L'Abbé**

Aubert (left) is one of the few Ph.D. students I had in logic, and Maurice is a logician too.   They are both Canadians; the picture was taken in Montreal in 1963.

112

113

G. R. MacLane

Gerald was the brother of Saunders Mac Lane; he was a complex analyst interested in Riemann surfaces, and in entire and meromorphic functions, and he served as chairman at Purdue.   Here he is in Boulder in 1963.

114

D. M. Stone

Here, in another Boulder picture, 1963, is someone whom the mathematical world knows by another name: she is Dorothy Maharam, the measure theorist.

115

W. F. Eberlein and A. H. Stone

Bill (left) was a functional analyst, who is best known for his characterization of weak compactness by weak sequential properties. He appears here out of chronological order because he is standing next to Arthur, a set-theoretic topologist, whose name appeared in the preceding picture. They are on their home ground, in Rochester, in 1972.

Zvonimir Janko

A single-minded simple groupie. This picture was taken in Sydney in 1964, a couple of years before his simple group was published; he and I just happened to be visiting Australia at the same time.

116

117

Kurt Mahler

Another Australian visitor in 1964, Mahler was an expert amateur photographer, a mediocre bridge player, and an outstanding analytic number theorist. A fascinating result he is credited with is the transcendentality of the number whose symbol in decimal notation is indicated by

0.1234567891011121314151617181920212... .

R. V. Churchill

This is the first of a group of nine pictures taken in Ann Arbor in 1964. Ruell was a member of the old guard, famous for best-seller textbooks on what might be described as engineering complex function theory and engineering Fourier series.

118

119

H. M. Stark

Harold was near the beginning of his career in 1964, a junior member of the Michigan faculty. He is a number theorist, and number theorists were sprouting all over the place in Ann Arbor in those days. His first spectacular work on the possible class numbers of certain imaginary quadratic number fields appeared a couple of years later. Both that work and its successor were part of what seemed to be a tight race: the same results were obtained independently and almost simultaneously by Alan Baker in Cambridge.

120

P. M. Cohn

Paul was one of the many Michigan visitors during the academic year 1964–1965. (The ones I have pictures of appear here in alphabetical order.) He is an algebraist who is interested in universal algebra, among other things. I shouldn't think he wants people to confound him with Paul Cohen whose fame rests on proving the independence of the continuum hypothesis, among other things.

Harold Davenport

Another number theorist, tending to be the analytic kind. One of his early results was that all but finitely many positive integers are sums of 16 or fewer fourth powers. He was English, very English. When he took a taxi to our house on Berkshire Road in Ann Arbor, his driver had a bit of trouble understanding his request to be driven to Barksher Road.

121

122

Louis Nirenberg

A long time member of the Courant Institute, a specialist in elliptic differential operators, pseudodifferential operators, Fourier integral operators, and other such modern outgrowths of classical hard analysis.

123

L. S. Pontrjagin

Pontrjagin is blind and has been so since he was 13. He is a great man but not a good guy. The impressively large quantity and outstandingly high quality of his mathematical contributions have resulted in his having a great deal of influence in the mathematical world of the Soviet Union, and it seems to be a matter of record that he is strongly antisemitic and that he allows such views to influence his professional judgments. He is a topologist, he has been very active in developing control theory, and he is most famous for the duality theorem that bears his name, the one about locally compact abelian groups. His book on topological groups is beautiful and readable; there are treatments that are more up to date, but even fifty years after its first appearance it might still be the best place to learn the subject from. There is a nasty review of it by Freudenthal (#52), reading almost like a personal attack, that appeared in the Nieuw Archief voor Wiskunde in 1940. The review occupies six printed pages and includes a long bibliography. Its main complaint is that the book does not give adequate credit to all the developers of the theory; in seven different places Freudenthal mentions works of his own to which Pontrjagin did not refer.

Alfréd Rényi

Known to many by his Hungarian nickname, Buba was an excellent probabilist, a heavy smoker, a vivacious raconteur, and the devoted father of his daughter Zsuzsi. One performance that he gave several times was a public reading of a dialogue (that he had written) on the nature of mathematics; he spoke one of the two parts and Zsuzsi the other.

124

125

Andrzej Schinzel

Another of the number theorists, this one from Poland, whom LeVeque and Lewis and their fellow conspirators liked to surround themselves with.

H. O. A. Wold

Some statisticians regarded him as one of them, but whether you call it statistics or measure theory or the theory of linear prediction, the ideas of which the Wold decomposition theorem is a part will live longer than most of us.

126

Mainly meetings,
the middle 60's

127 – 163

127

Will Feller

Will was an ebullient probabilist who spoke loud and fast and brilliantly most of the time in a heavy Yugoslav accent. When what he said wasn't brilliant, it was charming nonsense—amusing, and emphatic, and orthogonal to the facts. He worked very hard on his two-volume book on probability, which turned into the standard text in the subject. The book is difficult to find anything in, but it's worth a try; when you find something, it is rewarding. This picture was taken in Princeton, where I stopped on my way to the Amherst meeting of the AMS in 1964.

128

129

Joanne Elliott

Joanne is a Feller disciple, who worked for a while with the hush-hush Institute for Defense Analyses (I am pretty sure I have that right, plural and all) in Princeton. That's where this picture was taken, the same day as the preceding one.

R. H. Fox

Ralph was a topologist who was perhaps best known for being a knot-theorist; he was also a concert caliber piano player, and, incidentally, one of the best Go players in Princeton.

A. W. Tucker

A topological disciple of Lefschetz's, Al later became a combinatorialist, and incidentally chairman at Princeton. He has two sons, Tom and Alan, who are mathematicians. Their mother, born Alice Curtiss, is the daughter of a mathematician (D. R. Curtiss whom I knew as chairman of the department at Northwestern back in the 30's and 40's), the sister of a mathematician (Johnny Curtiss, #255, executive director of the AMS in the 1950's), and the widow of a mathematician (Ed Beckenbach, #541).

130

131

A. R. Amir-Moez and Abe Gelbart

Ali (left) has been a linear algebra enthusiast for much of his professional life. Abe's early work (on generalized analytic functions and compressible flows) was done jointly with Lipman Bers (when they were both at Syracuse); since then he has filled various administrative positions (such as chairmanships and deanships). This is the first of a batch of pictures taken at the 1964 AMS meeting in Amherst. The meeting was a great success from every point of view, including the point of view of one looking for snapshots that would be interesting to look at twenty and more years later.

S. A. Amitsur

A cheerful mathematician from Israel with a highly visible effect on commutative ring theory: there is an Amitsur complex and there are Amitsur cohomology groups.

132

133

T. W. Anderson and J. W. Tukey

This is a statistical conspiracy. Ted (left) can be counted on to do multivariate statistical analysis and time series most of the time, but John likes to hop around and drop pearls of wisdom in many subjects. His first work (titled *Convergence and uniformity in topology*) was ultra-pure, his statistical contributions are many (most of them in collaboration with others), and another concept that his name is associated with is the celebrated fast Fourier transform.

134

R. G. Bartle, J. V. Finch, S. P. Lloyd, and Herman Meyer

Bob (front right) is an analyst who used to consider integrals with respect to abstract-valued measures; his name appears on the title page of the book that is known as Dunford-Schwartz for short. More than once when Mathematical Reviews had editor trouble Bob was called on to step in and run that show. John (front left) is a Chicago Ph.D. who sat in on some of my courses there and with whom I had many cups of coffee between classes. He spent his teaching life at Beloit, and it horrified me to learn recently that he has already retired—nobody younger than I should be allowed to do that. Stu (rear left) has been with Bell Labs ever since I've known him. Herman (rear, between Finch and Bartle) is now retired from the University of Miami. He has many friends in common with another mathematician Meyer, W. H. L. Meyer of Chicago, known as Herman. The friends used to refer to the Chicago man as Herman the Lean and to the Miami one as Herman the Fat. Sorry, Herman, that's how it was, but I doubt that it comes as a surprise to you after all these years. I have no idea who the man at rear right is.

E. E. Floyd

Ed is a topologist, in the past a frequent collaborator of Pierre Connner; they both liked fixed points and periodic maps. More recently Ed has been administering: he is Provost of the University of Virginia.

135

136

L. R. Ford

Not the same as L. R. Ford: this one is Senior, the father of Junior (also a mathematician). He, Senior, studied continued fractions, and Les, Jr., has written about flows in networks (with Fulkerson). Senior was also editor in chief of the American Mathematical Monthly when I was young.

138

137

P. J. Freyd

Peter believes in categories, and abelian ones at that; he thinks they are algebra, and, in particular, he thinks they are good mathematics.

Mary-Elizabeth Hamstrom

Mary-Elizabeth (you have to say all that every time you speak to or about her) is a member of a non-empty but small set: the set of female R. L. Moore topologists whose Ph.D. mentor was R. L. Moore himself.

139

G. A. Hedlund

Gus is one of the earliest ergodicists. He studied the ergodicity of the geodesic flow on manifolds of constant negative curvature, he collaborated extensively with Marston Morse on something they called symbolic dynamics, and later with Walter Gottschalk on topological dynamics. He has been at Yale forever.

Solomon Lefschetz

Lefschetz was a colorful, charismatic, cantankerous character; it was impossible not to love him or hate him. He worked on algebraic varieties, mainly on topology (and was one of the early developers of homology theory), has a fixed point theorem of his own, and toward the end of his career decided to add Spanish to the several languages he spoke fluently, spent quite a bit of time in Mexico, and began writing papers on differential equations.

140

A. S. Householder

Alston and I share an interest in linear algebra, but we differ in that he wants to make it useful, and he succeeds.

141

I. J. Schoenberg and H. W. E. Schwerdtfeger

Iso (right) has been active in some hard parts of mathematics (such as interpolation theory involving splines and things) and continues to think and to produce long after retirement. He is, by the way, the son-in-law of Landau and a relative (but I don't know how) of the composer Arnold Schoenberg. Hans likes geometry, and matrices, and the connections between the two subjects.

142

J. L. Walsh

Joe studied approximation, in the complex domain, by systems of orthogonal polynomials, and there is also a family of (real) orthogonal functions named after him. A very small item among his claims to fame is that he is my mathematical grandfather: he was Joe Doob's Ph.D. supervisor. His own supervisor was G. D. Birkhoff (who is the biological father of Garrett Birkhoff of lattice fame). I have before me a xerox copy of the first few pages (handwritten) of Joe Walsh's 1920 Ph.D. thesis. In the preface he acknowledges that Part I was suggested by Bôcher, but he gives most of his gratitude to Birkhoff. To continue the genealogy, Birkhoff's mathematical father was E. H. Moore (who should never be confused with R. L. Moore). And that's the end of the Amherst, 1964, pictures; the next batch is from 1965.

143

144

Alex Rosenberg

The year 1965, presented here not strictly chronologically, gave me several interesting visitors to Ann Arbor, and Alex was one of them. The pipe is O.K., it was more or less standard equipment, but the smile is rare; see also #111. Alex was at Cornell for a long time, and then he moved to Santa Barbara where, the last I heard, he was chairmanning.

R. H. Nevanlinna

Rolf Nevanlinna's most famous work is known as the Nevanlinna theory; it is about the distribution of the values of meromorphic functions.

145

F. V. Atkinson

Another Ann Arbor visitor here, Atkinson's interests are close to mine; his name was made famous by Atkinson's theorem, a characterization of Fredholm operators.

146

Paul Turán

Paul was mainly a number theorist, interested in, for instance, the frequency of prime numbers in arithmetic progressions. He sometimes collaborated with Erdös (as who didn't?).

147

148

Vera Sós

Vera's picture belongs here even if it wasn't taken in Ann Arbor in 1965, but in Hungary in 1980— she is Paul Turán's widow. A mathematician in her own right, her specialty is combinatorics, and the Hungarian pronunciation of her last name is as if you said the word "show" twice, but stopped before the second time you came to the vowel:"show-sh".

P. P. Orlik

Peter's picture belongs here because, like his two predecessors, he too is Hungarian. The picture was taken in Ann Arbor in 1965, but usually he does his topology in Madison.

149

150

H. B. Mann

A mathematician active in more genuinely different parts of mathematics than is usual, Mann's interests included number theory (he won the Cole prize for his work on the so-called alpha-plus-beta hypothesis, having to do with the density of the sum of two sets of integers) and statistics (having to do with sampling problems and the design of experiments). Here, in 1965, he is in Miami.

151

Einar Hille and R. S. Phillips

Einar (left) wrote a book on semigroups. Ralph read it, and added to it, and the ultimate result was the well-known hyphenated Hille-Phillips book on functional analysis and semigroups. Hille's first name is pronounced like the middle part of "main-artery". Both men are known for reasons other than their joint book. Hille, for instance, collaborated with Tamarkin on hard classical analysis, and Phillips with Peter Lax on scattering theory.

152

J. S. Frame and P. D. Lax

J. Sutherland Frame (left), usually called Sud, has worked mainly on matrices and group theory. Before retirement he was an active member of the mathematical community, and, on a more local level, he was head of the mathematics department at Michigan State for 17 years. Peter is a leading PDE advocate, and he was president of the AMS for a couple of years.

153

Anneli Lax

Anneli is an outstanding mathematical editor (look at any volume of the New Mathematical Library) and, incidentally, Peter's wife. The picture was taken at the Ithaca meeting of the AMS in 1965.

Claude Chevalley

Chevalley was a first rate algebraist, a heavy smoker, and an indifferent but forever optimistic Go player. This picture of him was taken in Dundee, at the April 1965 British Mathematical Colloquium, where he was one of the featured speakers.

154

155

D. G. Kendall

David's measure theory, originally done at Oxford, became more and more useful as the years went by; he moved to Cambridge and became one of the leading statisticians of Great Britain. In this picture he is in Dundee.

156

V. G. Boltjanskii

In the spring of 1965 I went to Russia and the next four pictures, including this one, were taken there. Boltjanskii has worked in different things, such as topological Boolean algebras and (mainly) optimal control, and he was extraordinarily hospitable to me, taking me on a day's excursion to see some of the beauties of the countryside near Moscow. It wasn't his fault that there was a blizzard on May Day and that on May 4, when our excursion took place, it was both slushy and icy underfoot and mainly icy in the air.

157

158

M. A. Naimark

Mark Aronovich, the great "normed rings" man (they are called Banach algebras nowadays), was friendly and hospitable though he was just recovering from a stroke (he died not much later). He was a kind man as well as a great man.

S. V. Fomin and I. M. Gelfand

Some of the mathematical interests of Sergei Vasilievich (left) were always close to some of mine (measure and ergodic theory); he supervised the translations of a couple of my books into Russian. We had corresponded before we met, and it was a pleasure to shake hands with a man instead of reading a letter. Three or four years later he came to visit me in Hawaii, and it was a pleasure to see him enjoy, in contrast to Moscow, the warm sunshine. Israel Moiseevich is a deservedly famous all around mathematician who knows and is active in a frighteningly large amount of mathematics. His most recent interest, which he has been cultivating for several years by now, is in molecular biology. The picture was taken just behind Fomin's house in Moscow.

V. A. Rohlin

Vladimir Abramovich's name is sometimes transliterated as Rokhlin;
for sure, the h is not silent. He has been both an ergodicist and
a topologist (in that order). The picture was taken in front of the
elegant Hotel Astoria in Leningrad; the photographer's shadow is
more or less intentionally a part of it.

160

Géza Fodor and Attila Máté

On the way home from Russia in 1965 I stopped in Hungary and met Fodor (left). He studied large sets and their cardinal numbers, and he was proud of Attila, the young prodigy he had discovered. Attila has branched out, and grown older, since then. Classical analysis is among the subjects he has been studying, and, for instance, he was one of the first to digest and to explain to the rest of the world Carleson's solution of the du Bois Reymond problem concerning the convergence of Fourier series of continuous functions.

Hartley Rogers

The 1965 Ithaca meeting has already occurred in these pages, and that's where the last few pictures of this batch come from, and, in particular, that's where I caught Hartley. He is a double-threat man, at least: he has worked on both logic (studying effective definability and computability via recursive functions) and probability-statistics.

161

H. F. Bohnenblust

Boni was at Princeton when I was young; he didn't move to CalTech till much later. The notes on his real variable course, mimeographed and paper bound, were a best seller among graduate students of my generation; they were clearly written and beautifully organized. He speaks with a charming Swiss-French accent and used to think he could play Go.

162

163

W. W. Comfort

Wis does scary mathematics (like Stone-Čech compactifications), acts as associate secretary of the AMS, and knows a lot. When in connection with acting as editor of the *Monthly*, I needed advice on knotty mathematical-diplomatic problems, I turned to Wis, whose unofficial title was associate editor in charge of wisdom.

Irvine to Budapest, more 60's

164 – 197

164

Sigurdur Helgason

Sig is from Iceland, where, I am told, there are hardly any trees. To show off the beautiful countryside, we drove him around the woody hills of Michigan, but he didn't become ecstatic. "You can't see the scenery" he said; "all these trees are in the way." The mathematics he does is hard analytic geometry: symmetric spaces and Radon transforms and the like. He is blessed with a seemingly perpetual baby face; when this picture was taken (in Miami in 1966) he was 38.

J. D. Monk

Don is a logic type, or, to use language that is more dignified and accurate, he is interested in set theory. I was visiting Miami in the winter of 1966, and that's where this picture was taken.

165

166

A. D. Wallace

Alexander Doniphan Wallace, Don for short, was an extrovert. He was good-natured, but he liked to tell you where to get off, and then he liked it if you stood up to him. He was chairman at Tulane when I visited there once, and he bounced around quite a bit in that part of the world, having been associated with both the University of Miami and the University of Florida. His mathematics was topological semigroups, a theory that, to hear him tell it, had depth and importance equal to those of the theory of topological groups.

R. R. Goldberg

Dick indulges in Fourier transforms. When I first knew him he was at Northwestern, but he moved to Vanderbilt and became chairman there.

167

R. S. Palais and F. P. Peterson

Dick's mathematical interests (he is at the left) include Morse theory in infinite-dimensional spaces. He was a trustee of the AMS for a while, and at about that time he fell in love with computers. Nowadays he is an expert on technical word processors; he is the one who wrote a series of articles on them in the Notices. Frank is a topologist, and for a long time treasurer of the AMS, and, as such, ex officio a member of the Board of Trustees.

168

Trevor Evans

Another ardent believer in semigroups; when last seen he was chairmanning at Emory.

169

Leonard Carlitz

A conspicuously prolific number theorist at Duke; the 1965–1972 *Mathematical Reviews* index volume, for instance, lists over 150 of his papers.

170

171

W. G. Bade

Bill too has his name on the title page of Dunford-Schwartz; he is a functional analyst at Berkeley. Pronounce his last name in two syllables.

Karel de Leeuw

Another ex-Chicago student, Karel was a modern analyst (interested, for instance, in things like extreme points in H^1), an unusually nice guy, easy and pleasant to be with, a good teacher, and a conscientious student adviser. In 1978 he was brutally murdered by an ex-student with an unjustified grudge. In his memory, Stanford, where he worked, has established a lectureship bearing his name. This picture was taken at a large analysis conference at Irvine, in the spring of 1966.

172

173

B. R. Gelbaum, Einar Hille, Meyer Jerison, and G. L. Krabbe

Another Irvine picture. Reading from left to right it shows Hille, Jerison, Krabbe, and, just barely, the back of Bernie Gelbaum's head.

174

R. A. Kunze

Ray, who likes unitary representations of things, was another active participant at the conference; later he moved to Irvine "permanently" (as that word is used in academic circles). Now he is in Georgia.

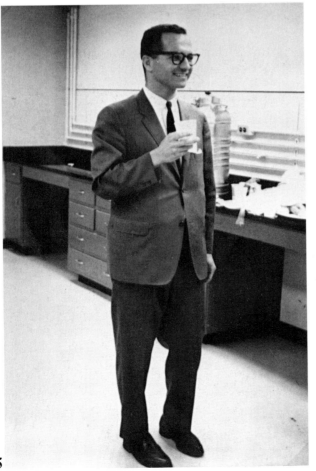

E. O. Thorp

Till about the early 1960's Ed, a member of the faculty at Irvine at the time of the conference, used to write papers on compact operators and on vector topologies. After that he started writing papers on subjects such as a favorable side bet in Nevada baccarat and a favorable strategy for twenty-one. He is known to many non-mathematicians as the author of *Beat the dealer*, a book describing his counting system of winning at blackjack. Rumor has it (and the rumor was strongly supported by newspaper stories at the time) that Ed's theory was more than just a theory for him: he put it to work and became moderately wealthy. Subsequently, the rumor goes on, he applied the same kind of reasoning to the operations of the stock market, and became wealthier.

Jesús Gil de Lamadrid, C. S. Herz, and Bernard Russo

Analysts all, at the Irvine conference: Carl is in front, Jesús is getting coffee, and Bernie is at the left.

176

J. A. Ernest

As a mathematician, John is a topological groupie who also knows and cares about von Neumann algebras. He has strong convictions outside mathematics too, convictions about the rights of women and convictions about peace being preferable to war. At the time of the Irvine conference, and for many years after, John was at the University of California in Santa Barbara. Since then, however, his peace convictions have influenced his career, and he is now working for the Center for International Security and Arms Control, at Stanford.

177

178

R. L. Bourgin, M. L. Curtis, and Eldon Dyer

I did a lot of travelling in the spring of 1966, and some of it took me to Texas. David Bourgin (#302) was still alive then (retired from Illinois, he was active at the University of Houston), and this picture was taken next to the swimming pool in his back yard. Eldon, a convinced topologist, is at left, Mort, another one, is sitting next to him, and David's wife Cherie (pronounced Sherry) is at the right.

Paul Lorenzen

He is a confirmed logician with whom I've had several friendly arguments about how to do mathematics. Here, in Austin, where he was visiting, he is happily waving the calculus book he wrote that had just appeared.

179

Eugenio Calabi

Gene does differential geometry, semisimple Lie groups, and other such hard things.

Emil Grosswald

His main work is the kind of number theory that has to do with the kind of functions such as zeta.

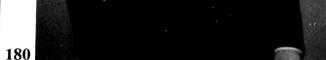

Walter Koppelman

He did things like singular integral equations at the University of Pennsylvania. He was not an easy man to write a thesis with; several graduate students had started to work with him, but none had ever finished. One whose thesis Walter had refused to accept (a decision that Oscar Goldman, chairman at the time, would not overrule) became murderous. He came to a colloquium talk a few minutes after the beginning, by a door next to the podium, shot and killed Walter, shot and injured Oscar Goldman (both of whom were sitting in the front row), ran out, and shot and killed himself.

182

183

R. J. Duffin

Dick was a physicist when I first knew him, but then he became a combinatorialist who just happens to be infinitely better informed about physics than you would expect a combinatorialist to be. This picture was taken on the Eastern part of my 1966 travels, in Pittsburgh.

184

Zeev Nehari

Complex function theory, and, in particular, conformal mapping was one of his interests; several of his papers studied the Bieberbach conjecture.

185

S. S. Shatz

Steve spells his name without a "c", but many people don't. He writes about sheaves and schemes and the cohomology of elliptic curves.

H. S. Wilf

Herb used to do numerical analysis and such like things; witness his book titled *Finite sections of some classical inequalities* (which I am proud to have had a hand in, having been the Ergebnisse editor who invited him to write it). Then he became more and more discrete, and now he is an expert on combinatorial matters, and, incidentally, he is editor of the *American Mathematical Monthly*.

186

187

Chung-Tao Yang

His specialty is topological groups and how they act on spheres. Hilbert's fifth problem is about the action of topological groups, and Yang was the one chosen to report on its solution at the 1973 conference on the Hilbert problems in De Kalb.

188

Gerard Washnitzer

When I met Jerry he was a graduate student; by the time I took this picture he had become a professor at Princeton, with a luxurious leather easy chair in his offfice. He hasn't resolved the Riemann hypothesis yet, but, because he isn't always lounging in an easy chair, we now know more about the Riemann-Weil hypothesis than we used to.

189

Ákos Császár

He is Hungarian, but his topology looks more Polish. The word "syntopogeneous" plays a fundamental role in several of his papers. I caught him in Budapest on the Hungarian part of my 1966 travels.

190

Géza Freud

Another Hungarian, also caught in Budapest. He was an analyst interested in interpolation, he emigrated to the U.S., and that is where, prematurely, he died.

192

P. S. Muhly

I knew Harry (H. T.) Muhly, Paul's father, a professor at the University of Iowa, a commutative algebraist of recognized quality. When I first met Paul (he was a graduate student at the time) I quickly asked, and I learned that he was Muhly's son. By now, since Paul became a professor at the University of Iowa, a functional analyst of recognized quality, most people think of Muhly as Paul's father.

191

László Kalmár

To catch this next Hungarian I had to go to Szeged. He was a logician who solved certain cases of the decision problem for the first order predicate calculus, and who was, in his lifetime, the acknowledged leader of Hungarian logic.

Alfred Schild

Alf was another Einstein assistant, a relativist by profession. This picture was taken in Ann Arbor on his 45th birthday.

193

194

195

D. S. Scott

Dana was a logic student of Tarski's. For a short time he was my junior colleague at Chicago, and there was a time when he was in the philosophy department at Stanford. Later he accepted a chair in England, at Oxford as a matter of fact, but after a while he came back to the States and became a professor in the department of computer science at Carnegie-Mellon.

Melvin Henriksen

Mel's is another name that people frequently spell wrong (by putting a "d" in it). When this picture was taken he was chairman at what was then called the Case Institute (till it merged with a neighbor institution and became Case Western Reserve). His main mathematical interest is in function spaces consisting, frequently, of continuous functions.

196

A. J. and Marjorie Lohwater

Jack was a colorful man, an active one, whom some people considered difficult, but with whom I got along famously. We worked together when he was executive editor of *Mathematical Reviews* and I was chairman of the editorial committee. He ran a taut ship. This picture belongs to his Cleveland period. Mathematically his interest was in the cluster sets and the boundary properties of analytic functions.

197

A. A. Armendariz, S. K. Berberian, R. J. Crittenden, and W. J. LeVeque

This is the *Math Reviews* crew in the fall of 1966. They were not all active editors simultaneously, but three of the four served as executive editors for a while (the exception is Armando), and they served under each other in various combinations as associate editors. Bill LeVeque is at left, Sam (whose official first name is Sterling) is next, Dick Crittenden is peering around Armando, who is grinning happily. The picture was taken in Ann Arbor, at the *MR* office. Armando stayed on with *MR* for many years, and Bill went on to various administrative positions (notably chairman at Michigan and executive director of the AMS); Dick and Sam returned to academia in the ordinary, teaching, sense of the word. Sam is known for several graduate level texts, including one on measure theory and one on operator theory.

Mainly Michigan,
the second half of the 60's

198 – 228

198

Rudolf Carnap and Herbert Feigl

In the 1960's I kept bouncing in and out of Hawaii, and, as one of the dividends of that pleasant habit, I had a chance to meet others who were doing the same thing. The philosophy department at the University of Hawaii had ambitions, and one of them was along the lines of logic; that's how I had a chance to meet Carnap (left) and Feigl. They were philosophers, rather than mathematicians, but Carnap, at least, used to think about "symbolic logic" (the old fashioned name for mathematical logic), and it was interesting to meet bona fide members of the famous Vienna circle.

199

László Fuchs and Emma Mader

Another Hawaii visitor, Fuchs is an outstanding abelian groupie, and he doesn't seem to mind being welcomed by Emma, the wife of Adolf Mader (#274), the leading resident algebraist.

K. M. Hoffman

In those days, the spring of 1967, Ken was very much a part of the functional analysis circle, and his book on Banach spaces of analytic functions was hot stuff. Later he became more and more an administrator, including being chairman at MIT, and later still he became "our man in Washington", the lobbyist representing several mathematical organizations, with the impressive title of Director of Federal Relations.

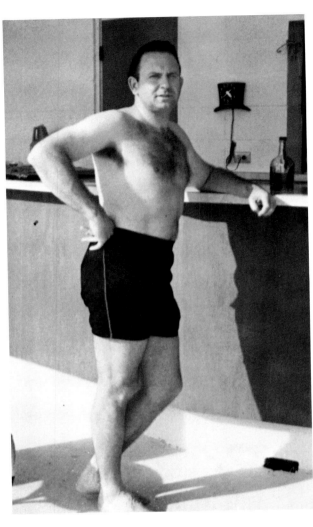

200

201

Shreeram Abhyankar

Abhyankar is an algebraic geometer who writes long long long papers on what he sometimes whimsically calls analytic geometry.

M. D. Fried

Mike does algebra and number theory and often a mixture of the two, a combination that tends to make algebraic geometers out of people.

202

203

Emil Artin

A great algebraist with a deep insight into many parts of mathematics and their interconnections, and a spectacular lecturer whose looks and whose show business style always reminded me of George Arliss.

W. B. Arveson

In 1967 Bill was not yet the trend-setter operator theorist he has become since then.

204

205

C. L. Dolph and Valentine Bergmann

Chuck Dolph (left) spent almost all his life at the University of Michigan; his main interest can be called applied mathematics. He is on his home territory in this picture; Valja is just visiting Ann Arbor. When I first met Valja, he was Einstein's assistant and he was a much more mathematical physicist than most who are so classified. He held a joint math-physics appointment at Princeton, and both sides were sure that really he belonged to them.

206

Lamberto Cesari and Ben Dushnik

The first I heard of Lamberto (left) he was an area theorist who solved some of Tibor Radó's hard problems. Later we were colleagues at Michigan and he was famous for his work on the asymptotic properties of the solutions of ordinary differential equations as well as for his contributions to control theory.

207

Robert Finn

Bob, here caught during a Michigan visit, is a Navier-Stokes kind of PDE applied mathematician at Stanford.

P. G. Hinman, R. C. Lyndon, and Alfred Tarski

This is a logic conspiracy. Peter (left) is a logician based at Michigan, and Alfred Tarski (center) is a visitor. Alfred was a chain smoker, who was sure that the habit didn't harm him because he didn't inhale; he lived to be 80. Roger, another Michigander, is mainly a group theorist, but he knows more about logic than many logicians do. The first story I heard about him was that in one of Quine's approaches to set theory, designed to eliminate all paradoxes, Roger was the one who found that the Burali-Forti paradox arose anyway.

208

R. M. Krause

Ralph gives money away. To be more exact, he is a program director (in charge of topology and foundations) of the NSF, and he is by now one of the old timers in the business. The picture was taken in Washington, D.C., in 1967.

209

210

Arthur Grad and W. H. Pell

Speaking of giving money away, here are two more who do (or, rather, did in the 1960's). Bill (left) was the chief NSF mathematical money man for a while, but Arthur preceded him and was better known to the people I knew. The job calls for a detailed acquaintance with the active mathematics and the active mathematicians of the day, as well as political and, when money is tight, diplomatic savvy. The picture was taken at the Toronto meeting of the AMS, and so were the ones that follow.

AMS Council 1967

The Council of the AMS, the elected body that runs the Society, gets together at every major meeting and sometimes in between. Here is a small fragment of the get-together at Toronto: Herbert Federer (left), H. L. Alder (talking to Herb), Everett Pitcher (secretary, seated at the center), and C. B. Morrey (president).

211

212

E. F. and R. C. Buck

Ellen (left) is a mathematician but Creighton is the one people usually think of when you say Buck: he is known as not only an active analyst but also as the author of a much used advanced calculus book.

H. C. Davis

Chan and I have many mathematical interests in common (notably operator theory), but he does many things that I don't, although I sometimes agree with him. He is a political activist who could never be described as a conservative. Here, at the Toronto meeting, he is against mathematicians doing war work.

213

B. R. Gelbaum and J. M. H. Olmsted

John (left) was one of the first people I met when I first went to Princeton (in 1939); being a knowledgeable graduate student he could be of tremendous help to a greenhorn Ph.D. just arriving at the center of the universe, and he was. His mathematical interest at the time was on measures on Boolean algebras. Bernie is another analyst; Banach algebras were his main interest for several years. They collaborated to produce a book that I love (*Counterexamples in analysis*); if you're learning or teaching real function theory, you should always have their book on your desk.

Abraham Robinson

Abby was both an applied mathematician and a pure algebraist and number theorist, but he is mainly remembered for being a non-standard analyst.

J. P. Williams

When I first met Jim he was a graduate student at Michigan and he registered in my functional analysis course. I was trying to run the course along R. L. Moore lines, and, accordingly, I asked those who had already been exposed to the subject to drop the course. It took a long time for Jim to forgive me for that exclusion, but we did become friends, and, years later at Indiana, colleagues. He was a dedicated operator theorist, and a popular member of the gang.

217

R. A. Rosenbaum

Bob served as editor of the *Monthly* for a couple of years (1967–1969), and that's what he was when this picture was taken; he was the immediate predecessor of Harley Flanders. Later he became Provost, and then Chancellor at his university (Wesleyan).

219

R. M. Solovay

Bob audited some of my lectures at the University of Chicago and then went on to become one of the most frightening set theorists in the world. He is the one who showed that, for all we know, every set of real numbers is Lebesgue measurable. (In a somewhat more honest formulation, what he proved was that the measurability of every set is as consistent with the usual axioms of Zermelo set theory as a lot of other statements that we cheerfully accept). The picture here was taken in Ann Arbor in 1968, as were several of the ones that follow.

218

W. T. Tutte

One of the four collaborators who produced a famous and often cited paper on squaring the square: the other three are R. L. Brooks, A. B. Smith, and A. H. Stone (#115). Tutte stayed in the combinatorics business and became one of the leading graph theorists of the world.

220

Paul Erdös

Paul can count better than anyone else. He is famous as a number theorist, set theorist, combinatorialist, geometer, and, in general, problem solver par excellence. He is also a world traveller who rarely stays anywhere for more than a week or two. How he manages to live that way is a mystery to some of his friends, but manage he does, and on a pretty good scale too. He has offered many cash prizes ($5.00 here, $1000.00 there) for the solution of outstanding problems, and he pays up like a gentleman. He doesn't usually look as relaxed and smiley as he does here.

Leo Moser

Leo loved problems: he invented them, he lectured about them, and he published many of them, and many of their solutions as well, in the *Monthly*. He was a combinatorialist by religion, a prolific collaborator, and, incidentally, an expert on puns and limericks.

221

Alexandra Bellow

She first became known to the mathematical world as Alexandra Ionescu Tulcea, a Romanian mathematician married to and frequently collaborating with the other Romanian mathematician whose name she bore. She works on what are called lifting theorems, in ergodic theory. The picture was taken the hour after she gave a colloquium lecture in Ann Arbor, in 1968. By well established tradition the talk was followed by a cocktail party and a dinner, and a part of the tradition was that these events were (or were to be interpreted as) professional occasions, not social ones. A consequence of the tradition was that spouses were not invited. (The argument ran like this: nine or ten people at dinner is nearly too large already—twice that many makes shop talk totally impossible.) When some of the spouses saw this picture (after the event), they were more than usually incensed at the kind of "stag parties" that they were excluded from.

Starting with the speaker (who, by the way, is called Gugu by her friends, and who is now married to the novelist Saul Bellow) and proceeding counterclockwise, the others are: Shaul Foguel, visiting Michigan from Israel; Ron Douglas and Allen Shields, Michigan faculty; Larry Wallen, visiting Michigan from Hawaii; M.S. Ramanujan (called Ram—no relation), Carl Pearcy, and Don Darling, all Michigan faculty.

223

Jim Douglas

Jim is as Texan as anybody can be, but he has been a Chicagoan for quite a few years; his interests are in the kind of partial differential equations that applied mathematics suggests, and, frequently, in their numerical solutions.

224

D. G. Higman and Eduard Wirsing

This is a group theoretic conspiracy. Don (right) is the Michigander host; Wirsing, from Germany, is the visitor who studies growth properties of sequences of various kinds, including, for instance, the sequence whose nth term is the number of abelian groups of order n.

225

Heinz Hopf

This is the second (and perhaps the more important?) half of Alexandroff–Hopf, caught during a visit to Ann Arbor in 1968. His influence on topology was great during his lifetime and seems not to diminish as the years go by. He worked on singularities of vector fields, fiber bundles, the homotopy groups of spheres and of topological groups, and there are things called Hopf algebras. He was also an extraordinarily pleasant and kind man. His greatness and his gentleness attracted Ph.D. students to him, and a part of his mark in topology was made indirectly through them. He was, for instance, the Ph.D. supervisor of Hans Samelson (#598).

226

Hans Lewy

Michigan had a lot of exciting visitors that year, and Hans Lewy was not the least. He has done a lot of important work in differential equations, but the only one I usually remember is his spectacularly simple and totally original example of an equation with very smooth coefficients that has no solutions at all, not even the phony, generalized kind involving distributions.

B. L. van der Waerden

A Dutchman who spent much of his life in Germany, he worked in algebraic geometry, and, although most people don't know this, he dabbled in statistics also (on the two-sample problem). He is best known for his classic text *Modern algebra*; even before it was translated into English it was often the basis of many graduate courses in the U.S. It's still hard to beat.

227

M. H. A. Newman

Another Ann Arbor visitor, Max was one of the early leaders of British topology. He worked on the pathology of 3-manifolds and wrote a widely quoted book *Elements of the topology of plane sets of points* on the 2-dimensional case.

228

Mainly Europe,
1968

229 – 251

229

A. H. Clifford and P. F. Conrad

It was a busy travel year, 1968, and on one of my swings I saw some old friends at Tulane. Here are a couple of algebraic types among them: Al (right) knew about things like groupoids and semigroups, and Paul has thought a lot about lattice-ordered groups.

K. I. Gross

Ken was another member of the New Orleans set when I visited there, but not an algebraic one; most of his work is in harmonic analysis.

230

231

Komaravolu Chandrasekharan and G. W. Mackey

Chandra (left) does hard analytic number theory. He did it at the Tata Institute, in Bombay, for a while, and then moved to the ETH in Zürich. He enjoys knowing the ins and outs of all the mathematical world; at the height of his administrative powers he was president of the International Mathematical Union. He does not have the same name as and is, so far as I know, not related to the astrophysicist Subrahmanyam Chandrasekhar. George has been at Harvard for all his professional life doing group representations and (it's the same thing, really) quantum theory. Here they are in Chicago, in 1968. Marshall Stone had moved to the University of Massachusetts by then, but, to honor him on his 65th birthday, the Chicago mathematics department arranged a conference and that was the occasion of the half dozen pictures beginning with this one.

K. O. Friedrichs

Friedrichs's work was on hard, applied, functional analysis, involving elliptic and hyperbolic differential operators and the like.

232

233

234

George Glauberman

He knows all about groups, especially the finite ones, and he sometimes even condescends to loops.

Shizuo Kakutani and Tosio Kato

Two more analysts, but of different kinds. Although much of Kakutani's (left) work is on ergodic theory, whereas Kato's principal book is *Perturbation theory for linear operators*, they do nevertheless have a language in common.

235

J. E. Nelson

Ed does many things including probability, Laplace transforms, and unitary representations; having done them, he became a non-standard analysis convert.

André Weil

This is as good a place as any to insert the picture of one who has often been named a candidate for the world's greatest living mathematician. Despite the breadth of his knowledge and the power of his creativity, he has been fiercely competitive most of his life. Many fear his aggressive sharp tongue, but some, notably his few students, remember only his kind helpfulness. As a lecturer he can be as difficult as his mathematics. In one course on algebraic geometry, after a brave auditor complained that Weil didn't write enough on the board, and, in particular, that he didn't draw any pictures, Weil resolved to mend his ways. He strode into the room the next time, picked up the chalk, hit its point sharply against the board once, began: "Let P be a point in the plane ...", and spent all the rest of the hour lecturing, with the otherwise empty board, about the point P.

236

237

J. G. Clunie, W. K. Hayman, Antoni Zygmund, and A. C. Offord

In the summer of 1968 I went on an extended European tour, and this picture was taken that June in London, my first stop. From left to right: Jim and Walter are complex functioners; the back of the head belongs to Zygmund (#469), the great trigonometer; and Offord is at the right. Offord's subject is the hardest to describe: he is interested in both complex function theory and probability, and has worked on, for instance, the distribution of the values of a random function in the unit disk.

238

A. S. Besicovitch

He was known as Bessy and he was famous for his work on almost periodic functions and for his solution of the Kakeya problem (what's the smallest area in which a car can turn around?). He wrote a book on almost periodic functions in which he discussed the class discovered by Stepanov (S a.p.), the definition of Weyl (W a.p.), and the definition offered by Bohr, the original discoverer and developer of the theory; the latter he called u.a.p. (the "u" for "uniform"). The symbol B a.p. was reserved for the concept proposed by Bessy himself. The picture was taken in Cambridge.

J. W. S. Cassels

Tea is important in Cambridge. Despite his initials, Cassels is called Ian by his friends. He is a number theorist; he became Hodge's successor as the closest thing the Cambridge mathematics department has to a head.

239

Heini Halberstam

Heini is an analytic number theorist. He was chairman at Nottingham when this picture was taken. Later he emigrated and became head of the mathematics department at the University of Illinois. His name is well known not for his mathematical merit only, but also as one of the leaders in the battle against the depersonalized NSF support policy for mathematical research.

240

Albrecht Dold

A very algebraic kind of topologist, and for a long time the chief editor of the infinitely large collection of *Springer Lecture Notes*.

241

Béla Bollobás

He is famous for his work (and books) on graph theory, but, believe it or not, he began as a functional analyst. The picture was taken on his original home territory, Budapest.

242

243

Oberwolfach, old

The climax of that summer's European tour was an Oberwolfach meeting, and here is the charming old building that was declared to be too small and too un-modern to continue to live; it was torn down soon afterward. Walking toward you, almost visible, are (from left to right) Ted Rivlin, Harold S. Shapiro, and Paul Butzer, the one in charge of the meeting.

Oberwolfach, new

The new building was put up before the old one disappeared; when this picture was taken they were just across the driveway from each other.

Reinhold Baer and Marcel Brelot

Reinhold (right, background) has occurred in these pages before (#19). Brelot is a potential powerhouse: harmonic and subharmonic functions, the Dirichlet problem, and all like that.

P. C. Curtis

Phil knows one Banach algebra from another, but most of the time his heart seems to be in approximation theory.

247

246

Bruno Brosowski

The official title of the Oberwolfach session I was attending was something like "approximation theory and functional analysis", representing the interests (overlapping to be sure) of the two organizers, Paul Butzer and Béla Sz.-Nagy. Brosowski is from the Butzer, approximation theory, side.

248

I. I. Hirschman and Alexandre Ostrowski

Two more approximators, in alphabetical order from left to right. Izzy has a book (joint with D. V. Widder) called *The convolution transform*. Ostrowski too has a book, a celebrated and widely quoted calculus book that was never widely adopted in the U. S.—it was much too good. The number of different parts of mathematics to which Ostrowski made a contribution is impressive. His is one of the basic names associated with valuation theory, he wrote about quasi-analytic function classes, proved non-trivial theorems about convex functions and, change of pace, meromorphic functions, and identified and studied the phenomenon of overconvergence.

Jean-Pierre Kahane

Jean-Pierre is a student of group theoretic trigonometry: he studies group algebras and the Fourier–Stieltjes transforms of measures.

249

250

Jacob Korevaar

Everything about the Dutch language is hard for me, including the nicknames it uses; as far as I can tell, all Dutchmen are called Jaap or Joop. This one is Jaap, and one of the things he is an expert on is the Dirac delta function and its derivatives.

251

G. G. Lorentz

George does approximations; one of the concepts his name is associated with is the theory of ε-entropy.

Partly Hawaii, the end of the 60's

252 – 281

252

Madison 1968

My last big travel occasion in 1968 was the Madison meeting of the AMS; it was a large one and a good one, and this is the first of a bunch of pictures I took there. The four figures more visible than the ones behind them are, from left to right, Yitz Herstein, Jack Schwartz, Bill Browder, and Gianco Rota.

D. L. Bernstein

Dorothy has written on Laplace transforms and has a book on existence theorems in partial differential equations; in 1979–1980 she was president of the MAA.

253

254

Chen-Chung Chang

I first met C. C. at a summer institute on logic at Cornell in 1957; it was a pleasure to re-meet him in Madison. He is a model theorist (model–theorist?).

J. H. Curtiss and J. B. Rosser

Johnny (left and back) was a function theorist and for a while (1954–1959) executive director of the AMS. His family has been mentioned before (#130). Barkley (always called by his middle name) was one of the leading recursive logicians of his generation, and, curiously, at the same time he was a powerful and widely consulted applied mathematician. (One of his books has to do with the mathematical theory of rocket flight.) He realized that the techniques of modern logic are usually too subtle for the run-of-the-mill theorem prover and he tried to give the trade secrets away in his books *Logic for mathematicians* and *Simplified independence proofs*.

255

256

Deans

This picture is a feeble pun, but when I saw these four men together in Madison I couldn't resist taking their joint picture. They are, from left to right: Wimberly Royster, Lowell Paige, Bernie Gelbaum, and Deane Montgomery, and what they had in common at the time was that they were all deans—all but Deane, that is.

257

Hidegoro Nakano

The first thing I learned about Nakano was his work on what is called the multiplicity theory of normal operators; that was something that had a great deal of interest for me once, and in my study of the subject I followed in the footsteps of Nakano (among others). Toward the end of his life he became interested in the foundations of set theory and distributed many preprints on that subject, but the professionals seemed to regard his approach with impatient suspicion.

258

R. J. Walker

Bob was an algebraic geometer; his book on algebraic curves was a pleasant and readable gift to those of us who didn't really want to be experts.

Everett Pitcher

For Everett meetings of the AMS were work, hard work, before, during, and after: he has been Secretary of the Society since 1967 (#211).

259

260

Henry Scheffé

Henry was a statistician, and one of the subjects he was an expert on is sometimes referred to by the repulsive neologism "anova" (for analysis of variance).

A. H. Wallace

Andrew does smooth topology (like differentiable manifolds), writes books explaining what he knows, and likes to travel. He used to go to Iran, for instance, when that was easy and pleasant, and even learned quite a bit of Persian.

261

262

Helmut Hasse

In 1968 I moved to Hawaii and met Hasse, the great German number theorist and algebraist, who was a visiting professor there when I arrived; that's where this picture was taken. Hasse reached the compulsory retiring age while I was chairman, and the dean gave me the thankless job of telling him that he could not continue next year; the rules applied to visitors too. It was not an easy thing to do, partly because I wanted him to continue (his presence added a great deal of prestige to the department), and especially because Hasse believed that I, the bearer of the bad news, was in fact at least partially its cause.

263

P. J. Cohen

One of the advantages of living in the Hawaiian paradise was that it was easy to entice glamorous visitors to come for a week's visit and preach to the heathen. Paul (whose greatest fame comes from his work on the independence of the continuum hypothesis) was one of the first such visitors we had during my year there.

264

J. L. Challifour, William Gustin, and Andrew Lenard

In December 1968 I was interviewed for a job at Indiana, and this picture was taken just before the colloquium talk I gave at that time. The three most clearly visible members of the audience, who subsequently became my colleagues are: Gustin (front left), Andrew (next on the right), and John (extreme right).

J. B. Conway

This too was taken in Bloomington in 1968. John is not to be confused with J. H. Conway (#600); neither one would like that. This one is an operator theorist with whom I have many interests in common. He has written a best-seller on complex function theory, as well as a text on functional analysis and a research monograph on subnormal operators.

265

266

Václav Hlavatý

A prolific differential geometer who was retiring from Indiana just when I was going there. He published, among other things, a long (numbered) series of papers on the space-time curvature tensor. He used to send out reprints on each of which he had stamped a large ordinal number, the number of the item in his bibliography.

267

P. R. Garabedian and George Springer

George (left) was chairman at Indiana when I was being interviewed; he is the one who hired me. Paul was just visiting for a few days, possibly because someone had the idea that he too could be persuaded to move there, but he didn't do so. I met Paul when he was an undergraduate, a breath-takingly bright one; later he became a powerful analytic applied mathematician.

268

Albert Wilansky

I never found out why he is called Tommy, and I don't know what he was doing in Bloomington in December 1968 (another intervie-wee?), but he is and there he was. His mathematical interests stem from summability theory.

269

L. W. Cohen

In January 1969, I had already agreed to move to Indiana, but the academic year wasn't over yet, and the visitors who were invited earlier were still happily expected. Leon was one of them. As far as most mathematicians were concerned, he was "Mr. NSF" for a long time: he was the one you turned to if you wanted summer research money. He started out as a mathematician, of course, an analyst; the last teaching job he had was at the University of Maryland.

L. M. Milne-Thomson

One morning in Hawaii, the secretary of the mathematics department brought to my office a little scrap of paper to which was stuck an address label (an ingenious home made calling card) bearing the name of Milne-Thomson. Even to a purist like myself the name was famous; I thought of him as bearing the standard of classical British applied mathematics (such as hydrodynamics), and he was the author of a well-known text on the calculus of finite differences. He was retired when I met him, and travelling around the world; he stopped in Hawaii and at the university just for fun. He was a charming and cultured gentleman; it was a pleasure to shake his hand and to share a meal and a drink with him.

Basil Gordon

A leading number theorist who visited the University of Hawaii for a week, giving a series of lectures. Knowing him was profitable for me: in subsequent years I turned to him several times for help with number theoretic refereeing.

M. R. Hestenes

Magnus was a part of the Chicago crowd when I first met him, but he has been at UCLA for a long time. I associate his name with the calculus of variations, the old Bliss school.

273

Paulo Ribenboim

Paulo is a prolific writer of books on almost every aspect of algebra (fields, groups, modules, valuations) and number theory. He knows everything worth knowing about Fermat's last theorem (except the proof).

274

Adolf Mader and J. A. Wolf

Adolf (left) is a permanent fixture at Hawaii, an algebraic fixture; Joe, the visitor, studies curvature on Riemannian manifolds.

H. S. Bear

Don't ask me why Herbert S. Bear, Jr. should be called Jake, but he is. His picture is the last in this Hawaii bunch not because he was the last visitor during my term there, but because he was my last administrative duty. The dean told me to find the right person to replace me as chairman, and I proposed Jake. The picture shows him on his interview visit; a few months later he became the chairman.

275

Nachman Aronszajn

Aronszajn's most famous contribution, at least in the circles I move in, is his proof (jointly with Kennan Smith, #100) of the existence of non-trivial invariant subspaces for compact operators on Banach spaces. Here he is enjoying his cigar between lectures at the 1969 winter meeting of the AMS in New Orleans.

276

277

A. R. Bernstein

Allen is a logician, but his most famous work is, probably, his solution (jointly with Abraham Robinson, #215) of another long-standing open problem about invariant subspaces (one about square roots of compact operators).

E. A. Coddington

One of the most widely quoted books on differential equations is the one Earl wrote jointly with Norman Levinson.

278

279

AMS Council 1969

The Council takes a coffee break during its 1969 New Orleans meeting. Gene Isaacson is at left, in the back, and Murray Gerstenhaber and Oscar Zariski (right) are in front. Unrecognizable in the back center are Kurt Friedrichs, facing forward, and Jürgen Moser with his back to the camera. (Oscar was then President of the AMS. He hated the job; it took too much time, it involved arduous paper-shuffling, and it forced him to accept compromises with the mathobureaucracy. He stayed away from it, in Italy, as much as he could and a little more.)

280

M. D. Morley

Mike is a logician, and I seem to have just caught him on the wing in New Orleans.

L. C. Young

Larry's mathematical genealogy is unexceptionable; he is the son of William Henry Young and Grace Chisholm Young, the first husband and wife partnership in the history of mathematics. His specialty comes from the calculus of variations (sometimes using the language of optimal control); he has a long numbered series of papers on extremal questions for simplicial complexes.

And that's the end of a chapter. The New Orleans meeting was the last one at which I represented Hawaii. In May of 1969 I moved to Indiana, and started travelling to other places and other meetings.

281

Based in Bloomington, the turn to the 70's

282 – 334

J. K. Hale
Almost the first thing I did after moving to Indiana was to go to a conference at a somewhat more than usually glamorous location, namely in Poços de Caldas, in the mountains a couple of hundred miles from Rio de Janeiro. That's where this picture of Jack was taken. His differential equations are sometimes not even linear.

282

Abel Klein
Abel was still a student at the Poços de Caldas conference; since then he has become an American and an established physics mathematician who studies quantum systems by means of associated stochastic processes.

283

284

Wolfgang Krull

The most glamorous mathematician at Poços de Caldas was undoubtedly the great Krull, the immortal algebraist (and, in particular, ring theorist).

285

Jacques Neveu

Jacques does probability and ergodic theory, and, although he is quite a bit younger than I am, I had him puffing when we walked up to "the Cristo", the large statue of Christ at the top of a steep hill.

G. L. Weiss

Guido is a harmonic analyst, a disciple of Zygmund's, who sometimes collaborates with Eli Stein (#513), another such disciple; they have worked, in particular, on the interpolation theory of operators. He and I keep bumping into each other at various places; this time, in the summer of 1969, it was in Eugene, Oregon.

286

287

288

Martin Barner

This picture of Barner was taken in Toronto, but his home territory is in Freiburg, just a few miles down the road from Oberwolfach, and he has in fact been the chief administrator of that delightful conference center for many years.

K. O. May

Ken was on his home territory (Toronto) when this picture was taken. He was an expert historian of mathematics.

T. Y. Thomas

Tracy was just retiring from Indiana when I arrived there. In some budgetary sense (but not in a mathematical one) I was his replacement. His specialty was applied mathematics, and he was in fact the founder of *The Journal of Mathematics and Mechanics* (which later became the *Indiana University Mathematics Journal*, and which, in turn, is sometimes misaddressed as the *Indian Journal of Mathematics*).

289

290

291

Morton Lowengrub

Mort is an applied mathematician who has collaborated quite a bit with Ian Sneddon on cracks. More recently he became administratively busy: he was chairman for a while and then became dean of research and graduate development.

Seymour Sherman

Slim knew about both the abstract kind of mathematics and the concrete kind, and in his later years (when he thought less about ordinal numbers than about probability) he became a vociferous advocate of applications. He was a big man, who often laughed, loudly, but rarely smiled.

292

W. F. Donoghue

One of my first assigned duties at Indiana was to take charge of the "Sesquicentennial Seminar". (The university was celebrating its 150th birthday that year). As a result we had many visitors rushing in and out of Swain Hall, and Bill, a popular numerical ranger (a part of operator theory to which he contributed) was one of them.

F. L. Gilfeather

Frank was not one of the visitors —he was a part of the home team that year working in operator theory. Since then he has become highly visible in Washington, having been connected with the NSF, the NAS, and other such wealthy organizations.

293

294

I. L. Glicksberg

Irving was caught working. His work in those days was on function algebras; since then he has even been known to dabble in control theory.

J. G. Glimm

In 1969 Jim was a C^* algebraist (interested in abstract Radon-Nikodým theorems, among other things) who knew a lot about physics; since then he has made such a name for himself in that direction that he can be called a C^* physicist.

295

Henry Helson

Henry is a member in very good standing of the operator community.

296

297

V. L. Klee

It's not quite fair to identify Victor with convexity, but at least it's looking in the right direction. Along the way (1971–1972) he was also president of the MAA.

298

B. L. Osofsky

Since Barbara does algebra, not functional analysis, she was a member of a smaller group that year; her talk was not to the Sesquicentennial Seminar but to the departmental colloquium. She likes rings and she sometimes calculates homological dimensions.

299

Y. A. Rozanov

Pesi Masani was on the Indiana faculty, and he was the one responsible for inviting Rozanov, a Russian probabilist, to pay us a visit.

R. L. Moore

An influential Texas topologist, a prolific producer of Ph.D. students, and a powerful developer and user of the Socratic discovery method of teaching (which is usually called the Moore method in Texas)—here he is in his office in Austin, in January 1970.

300

301

Joshua Barlaz and R. P. Boas

Barlaz (left) was a dedicated problem activist, intimately associated with the *Monthly* over a long period.   Boas is an all around analyst and mathematical craftsman: he has made his mark in, among other things, polynomials and entire functions, has written a beautiful little expository book (which he called *A primer of real functions*), has taught himself an amazing number of languages (including Russian and Hungarian) well enough to cope with their mathematical literatures, and has found time to be one of the early executive editors of *Math Reviews* and an innovative and memorable editor of the *Monthly*. Here they are at the San Antonio meeting of the AMS in 1970.

302

D. G. Bourgin and R. L. Bourgin

David was an energetic mathematician who was interested in topology among other things, a charming, cultured, and witty dinner companion, and a simply awful lecturer. He was already well launched on his career at Illinois when I was a student there. He and his wife Cherie (#178—very few people know that her name is Rose) were hospitable parent substitutes to a lot of bewildered young students; you could always count on meeting a few friends playing ping pong in the Bourgins' basement.

E. Dubinsky

Ed is nothing if not active. He is known to many as a political activist, not always on the most popular side; mathematically he has continued to be interested in functional analysis; and, in recent years, he has become famous (and popular) as a computer educator; many mathematicians became retreaded under his guidance and are now happily meeting the great demand for teachers of computer science.

303

304

W. T. Martin

Ted's mathematical start was in the theory of functions of several complex variables (he and Bochner, #67, collaborated on a book on that subject), but he became an administrator relatively early in life and is remembered by many as the chairman of the MIT mathematics department and the treasurer of the AMS.

P. E. Thomas

When Emery is not being a topologist, he is another AMS bigwig (a long time member of the Board of Trustees); here he is just enjoying the San Antonio meeting.

305

G. K. Kalisch

Gerhard is an analyst hovering between hard and soft, who is remarkable also for his finely tuned linguistic ear. His German is native, his French (I have been assured) is accent free, and if there is anything foreign about his English it's sure hard to spot.

306

E.W. Barankin

Some people might remember Eddie because of his work on unbiased estimation and sufficient statistics, but I remember him most fondly from his days when he was a graduate student at Princeton in 1941 and was one of the official note takers in my course called *Elementary theory of matrices*. That was the course out of which my book on finite-dimensional vector spaces grew. This picture was taken when Eddie visited Bloomington, in January 1970.

307

308

David Ruelle

Is he a physicist or a mathematician? Interested in the foundations of quantum mechanics, he knows enough about both subjects to be welcomed as a pro by both professions.

309

O. E. Lanford

This picture was taken in February 1970, when Oscar was one of the sesquicentennial visitors in Bloomington. Now he is a mathematician in California, but he moonlights as a physicist in France—or is it the other way around? The most recent evidence (a prestigious National Academy award for work in statistical mechanics) doesn't settle the question.

I. E. Segal

I have known Irving since the early 1940s, and was his colleague at Chicago for a while. His pure functional analysis has been leading him more and more into physics as the decades rolled by—C^* algebras, quantum physics, and then even cosmology.

310

L. M. Kelly

Roy is the main reason why year after year Michigan State kept producing a magnificent series of Putnam winners, both teams and individuals; he found them, he pushed them, he coached them, and he succeeded with them. This picture was taken on his home territory, East Lansing, in 1970.

311

Ergebnisse editors

The Ergebnisse series of research monographs has a small editorial board. At the time of its 1970 meeting in Bloomington it consisted of four people, and three of them are in this picture; the second from the right is Klaus Peters who, as a Springer inhouse editor at the time, was in charge of us all. The others are, from left to right, Reinhold Remmert, Béla Sz-Nagy, and, to the right of Klaus, Peter Hilton; the fourth member of the board was myself, behind the camera.

312

313

David Eisenbud

I knew David before he was born. His father, Leonard Eisenbud, is a mathematical physicist, who was a graduate student in Princeton when I first showed up there. David, photographed here during a Bloomington visit, became a purely algebraic pure mathematician.

314

Leon Ehrenpreis

In March, 1970, I visited Yeshiva University, and this is the first of four scalps I was able to collect there. Leon does hard analysis, such as finding "fundamental solutions" for differential operators with constant coefficients.

316

Martin Schechter

Martin too was at Yeshiva then. His elliptic differential operators look so useful that he is sometimes called an applied mathematician.

315

D. J. Newman

Don was at Yeshiva then too. He loves and works in many parts of mathematics, and he loves and solves many problems. His booklet, modestly called *A problem seminar*, deserves to be a best seller (and is as near to being one as a high level mathematics book can ever be).

H. N. Shapiro

This Harold Shapiro is not the same as the other Harold Shapiro (#563); the middle initials are important. This one does analytic number theory.

317

318–320

318

Konrad Jacobs

He knows everything about ergodic theory, whether it is topological or measure theoretic; here he is attending an ergodic meeting in Columbus.

319

H. O. Pollak

I don't know how much Henry knows about telephones, but he did (and directed) mathematical research for Bell Telephone till that company ceased to exist, and then did it a little longer anyway. He is a topnotch problem solver and dedicated problem advocate; he was president of the MAA in 1975–1976. Here he is at Lehigh University in the spring of 1970.

F. J. Weyl

Do the children of mathematicians often become mathematicians themselves by genetic inheritance, parental encouragement, or Oedipal competition? In any event Fritz (whose mother was horrified to hear her son Joachim called Fritz by his American contemporaries) followed in the footsteps of his father, Hermann Weyl, and published some long and difficult papers on analytic curves. One of them was in collaboration with his father, who had earlier written a book titled *Meromorphic functions and analytic curves*.

320

R. W. Beals
From Lehigh I hopped over to a brief Chicago visit, where I caught Dick, who believes in PDE's. He moved to Yale later.

321

322

P. P. Billingsley

Pat is a permanent fixture at Chicago. Call it probability, ergodic theory, or statistics—he does it all. Where does he find the time to be a professional caliber amateur actor?

323

B. E. Johnson and Joram Lindenstrauss

That was a busy year for me, 1970, but I did have time to touch base in Bloomington every now and then, and one of those times I caught a couple more distinguished visitors. They are both functional analysts: Barry (right) leans to algebra and analysis (the continuity of homomorphisms of Banach algebras) and Joram more to the geometry of Banach spaces.

Susan Chambers

The biggest event in my life in 1970 was a series of ten NSF supported lectures I was invited to give in June at TCU (Texas Christian University) in Fort Worth. This is the most notable picture from that session: I was told that Susan is the great great granddaughter of Gauss.

324

I. D. Berg and A. E. Nussbaum

Analysts both, definitely of the functional kind, both were attending the TCU conference. David (right) didn't believe me when I said that every Hermitian operator is a sum of a diagonal operator and a compact one, but after a while he not only discovered a proof for himself, but went on to solve the corresponding open problem for normal operators.

325

Joseph Diestel

In 1970 Joe wasn't yet the famous Banach spacer he has become since, but he could drink a lot more beer than I.

326

327

H. E. Lacey

Elton is a Banach spacer too, the author of one of the basic sources of information about the isometric theory of Banach spaces, and, incidentally, the father of a budding young mathematician.

328

Pasquale Porcelli

Despite his mellifluous Italian name, everyone called him Pat. He worked on topological algebra (spaces of analytic functions, rings of operators). He was not a prolific publisher, but he was a charismatic, dynamic, and forceful teacher. He was never in doubt about anything, and (as a consequence?) his students worshipped him.

329

C. R. DePrima and Andrew Sobczyk

Charlie (hovering at the right) attended the TCU conference as the official NSF "spy", or, in more dignified language, observer, sent to make sure that everything that was supposed to happen did indeed happen, and then to say so, to the NSF, in an official report. Shaking hands, Andy (pronounced Sob-chick) was a well-known part of the mathematical scene during the middle years of the century; his principal interest was in topological problems about function spaces. One of his memorable contributions is the Bohnenblust-Sobczyk theorem, which is the complexification of the Hahn-Banach theorem. (And this, by the way, is the last TCU picture.)

Jacques Dixmier

The next 1970 conference I went to was in a rather different part of the world, in Hungary. The only picture I got there was of Dixmier, one of the leading gurus of C^* algebras, and here he is, in Tihany. I was told that the x in his name is supposed to sound like an x: say dix-me-hay, but don't sound the h which I put in there only to make clear the intended vowel sound.

330

331

J. E. Brothers and W. P. Ziemer

Between conferences I sometimes spent time back at my home base in Bloomington, and here are a couple of my colleagues from there. Both John (left) and Bill could be described as geometric measure theorists, interested in objects such as minimal surfaces.

332

G. J. Minty

Another Indiana colleague, George was famous for his contribution to the theory of monotone operators; later he worked on more combinatoric notions, and, later still, he became a computer buff who loved to tell you more about your computer question than you ever thought you wanted to know.

G. L. Walker

Gordon was called Executive Director of the AMS, and he really ran the Society for many years. Presidents could come and go, but Gordon, as a permanent salaried employee, stayed on and on, and it was his job to carry out the policies of the Council and the Board of Trustees.

333

AMS, Executive Committee

The AMS is run by its Council, but the Council grew to be too unwieldy and found it necessary to elect an Executive Committee to which to delegate most of its detailed business. Here is a meeting of that committee, in Providence, in October 1970. Starting from the left and reading clockwise, the people you see are: Lincoln Durst, Sammy Eilenberg, Michael Atiyah, Cal Moore, Mort Curtis, Gordon Walker, and Bill LeVeque.

334

Bloomington, St. Andrews, and between, the early 70's

335 – 377

Stephen Heims

Since 1971 was not one of my travellingest years, more than half of its relatively few pictures were taken in Indiana. To avoid too scattered an effect, I'll begin by presenting them all together, before showing the few that were taken elsewhere. Stephen Heims came to interview me when he was preparing his book on the saintly Norbert Wiener and the fiendish John von Neumann (or at least that's the impression that his portraits gave to many readers). Love it or hate it, you should look at the book and at its scholarly but emotionally strong review in the *Bulletin of the AMS* (1983) by Marshall Stone.

M. G. Arsove

Maynard has been doing subharmonic functions and potential theory at the University of Washington for hundreds of years; here he is on a visit to Bloomington.

Hyman Bass

Hy is a leading algebraist, but when I met him, as a graduate student at Chicago, all that was predictable was that we'd be proud of him. He took a course in algebraic logic from me, in which I mentioned an unsolved counting problem one Monday (how many free monadic algebras on two generators are there?). By the time I arrived at the next meeting of the class, on Wednesday, Hy had the solution written on the board (namely 4,294,967,296, or in plain English 2^{32}); that solution, and the algebraic context it belongs to, became his first paper.

338

339

William Browder

There are three mathematical Browder brothers, but unfortunately, I have pictures of only two of them. Bill, the topologist, is the middle one in age, I believe, but he is shown first here just by the chronological accident of having been caught first.

J. K. Moser

After G. D. Birkhoff, ergodic theory became almost exclusively measure theoretic for a while, but in more recent times the classical (analytic and topological) dynamical systems have regained their place in the world, and Jürgen is one of the fomenters of this re-revolution.

340

Paul Révész

Paul was born as a probabilist, and although his stuff is sometimes done in departments that have the word "statistics" in their name, he is still an active contributor to pure probability theory—in Budapest, or Ottawa, or Vienna, or any one of many places where he is welcome.

R. O. Wells

Since almost everyone calls him Ronny, very few know that his initials stand for Raymond O'Neill. His mathematics is holomorphic everything: hulls, approximation, convexity. He has been known to think about complex geometry in mathematical physics, and he has a book titled *Differential analysis on complex manifolds.*

341

342

Herman and Jean Rubin

Herman was a graduate student at Chicago when I met him, and he was frighteningly bright and not shy. He knows not only statistics, his business, but a lot of modern analysis, and set theory as well; Jean, his wife, has set theory as her main business.

F. D. and P. T. Bateman

Paul is a number theorist, who was for a long time head of the math department at Illinois; Felice, his wife, is also a colleague of his, in the same department. Here they are slumming: number theory or no, they are attending a meeting of the Wabash Extramural Functional Analysis Seminar, in Crawfordsville, Indiana.

343

344

M. A. Arbib and M. H. Stone

In the spring of 1971 I visited Amherst, which is where Michael Arbib (right) is a big shot in computer science. Marshall has been one of my mathematical heroes ever since his Hilbert space book first appeared. (It's irrelevant, but does everyone know that he is the son of Harlan Fiske Stone, one time Chief Justice of the Supreme Court?) When he retired from Chicago he moved to the University of Massachusetts at Amherst, and that's where this picture was taken.

N. H. McCoy

Neal's books (especially the one on rings and ideals) were among the best sources of wisdom from which many of us learned algebra. This picture too was taken at Amherst.

345

346

R. M. Dudley, M. P. Gaffney, and Bertram Kostant

Dick (right) is a probabilist, Matt (center) is always a nice guy, but he was most popular when he was money-away-giver for the NSF, and Bert knows all about Lie groups and algebras and their representations.

347

Ruben Klein, R. T. Seeley, and J. T. Tate

Bob (right) does pseudo-differential operators, and John (left) is an outstanding number theorist and algebraist, a pupil and son-in-law of Emil Artin. The man in the center is Ruben Klein, the statistically inclined brother of Abel Klein (#283).

348

E. J. McShane

Jimmie belongs to the calculus of variations tradition, but he is an all around mathematician who contributed, among other things, to our understanding of abstract integration. He wrote a book on order-preserving maps and another one on exterior ballistics—not an everyday combination. He was president of the AMS in 1959–1960. Except that he was born in New Orleans (and sometimes still sounds like it), many years in Charlottesville have converted him into a genuine Virginian.

349

L. D. Pitt

Loren is a disciple of Will Feller's in probability; this picture was taken in Charlottesville.

350

F. T. Birtel

New Orleans is one of my favorite cities, and that's where I caught Frank. Mathematically he does Banach algebras from the complex function point of view—function algebras, uniform algebras, and the like—and he has been an associate secretary of the AMS for a long time.

351

J. A. Goldstein

Another Tulane shot: that's where Jerry looks for solutions of hard equations, such as stochastic differential equations, wave equations, and evolution equations. And that closes the year 1971.

D. L. Burkholder
Don does almost everywhere convergence in ergodic theory, and he does martingales in probability theory. Here he is on a Bloomington visit in 1972.

352

353

Avner Friedman
Avner is a prolific partial differential equator, who does, among other things, stochastic differential equations, with a very applied bent. Another Bloomington visitor, one whom Indiana had hoped to tempt to move there.

354

Leonard Gross
Lenny is a Chicago product—I knew him way back then. By the time of this picture he was established as an expert analyst in Hilbert space, and he was visiting Bloomington in that glamorous capacity.

355

Meyer Jerison

Jerry (as his friends insist on calling him) was a successful chairman of the math department at Purdue during one of Purdue's greatest periods of growth and improvement. He is the author (with Leonard Gillman, #460) of a book on rings of continuous functions, and he is proud of becoming known not as Jerison but as (David) Jerison's father. It wasn't hard to snap him in Bloomington: while I was book review editor of the *Bulletin* he visited me often and was a great help; when my tenure was over, he took the job.

356

C. L. Schochet

Claude was a patriotic topologist till he became seduced and became a patriotic C^* algebraist; he enjoys collaborating with Cal Moore (#558). He was easier than most to snap in Bloomington: that's where his job was in those days.

357

H. B. Keller

This picture was taken in Las Vegas in January 1972. It's easy to tell Herb apart from his brother (whose picture, out of chronological order, is the next one): they both have beards and they both do applied mathematics in California.

J. B. Keller

One difference between Joe and his brother is that this picture of Joe was taken in Bloomington in 1978. Joe's name is associated with, among other things, bifurcation theory. He has many other interests. One time I saw him he was fascinated by (and did serious thinking about) the problem of fair dice: which polyhedra have the property that when rolled at random all their faces are equally likely to end up at the bottom? ("Top" is hard to define sometimes, so why bother?)

358

359

C. L. Fefferman

Charlie doesn't have a high school diploma, but he became full professor of mathematics at the University of Chicago at the age of 22; I took this picture a year later when I gave a colloquium talk at Chicago. His forte is to do in many dimensions what classical analysts found hard enough in one; for that activity he received the Fields medal in 1978. He has also done spectacular work on the duality of H^1 and BMO, and he hasn't stopped yet.

Robert Fefferman

Bob is Charlie's kid brother, and his picture belongs here even though it was taken much later (in Bloomington in 1979). As far as fields of interest go, it is sometimes hard to tell the two of them apart; Bob too is interested in singular integrals, in the Calderon-Zygmund theory, and he even got into the H^1 versus BMO act (on the bidisc).

360

H. F. J. Löwig

I caught Löwig while I was visiting Edmonton in May 1972 (winter was just about over). I had known his name for a long time: one of the things he proved, with obviously the best possible proof, is that Banach spaces have well-defined dimensions—a proof that people have often rediscovered and applied to more and more general situations.

361

362

Edwin Hewitt and R. R. Phelps

Mathematically speaking, Ed (left) is harmonic and Bob is convex, but they are both mathematicians of broad vision for whom a one-word summary is an approximation at best. The picture was taken on their home stomping ground, in Seattle. It remains Ed's home stomping ground despite exciting announcements, which seem to come about every other year, that he has accepted a job in Utah, no, in Alaska, no, in Germany, no, etc.

363

Hugo Rossi

One complex variable is not enough for him. The picture was taken in Seattle, in May 1972.

364

J. M. Anderson

This picture, and the next half dozen, were taken at the 1972 St. Andrews colloquium, in July. The colloquium gathers every leap year and lasts a couple of weeks or so; it's one of the pleasantest and at the same time mathematically broadest conferences I know of. One of the participants that year was Milne (never James) Anderson who does complex function theory, and, even though his job is in London by now, sounds more Scottish than any Dallasian sounds Texan.

A. M. Davie

Sandy is quiet but powerful. He not only does beautiful mathematics and solves hard problems (such as the one about the invariant subspaces of the so-called Bishop operators), but he is also superb at understanding the mysterious solutions of others and transcribing them so that lesser mortals can understand them too. That's what he did with Enflo's solution of the so-called approximation problem for Banach spaces. Since his home base is Edinburgh, it was easy for him to come to the St. Andrews Colloquium.

365

James Eells

Jim didn't have far to come either; he was based in Britain in 1972. His work is mainly in differential geometry.

366

367

Frank Harary

Frank was a colleague of mine at Michigan. He does graph theory—or is it called combinatorics?—in any event, if it can be counted, preferably as a function of n, he wants to count it.

Masatake Kuranishi

Another colleague of years before, Kuranishi's time overlapped mine at Chicago; it was pleasant to bump into him again in St. Andrews. He does complex analytic structures and Lie groups and such. Some of his linguistically untalented friends in Chicago simplified his name and just referred to him as Crunch.

368

369

George Lusztig

In 1972 he wasn't quite as famous as he has become since, but the people who knew about his work on groups knew that he would be; in 1985 he got the Cole prize for his work on the representation theory of finite groups of Lie type.

370

371

Nora and Frank Smithies

Frank is sometimes called the father (or grandfather) of British functional analysis. He was a Reader at Cambridge for many decades, till he became a Reader Emeritus. Being Scottish by birth gave him an extra incentive for being a regular attendant at St. Andrews colloquia, always accompanied by his wife Nora.

E. M. Luks

We are out of St. Andrews now; this picture of Gene was taken in 1972 while I visited Bucknell, where he was on the faculty at the time. He used to think about Lie algebras and cohomology, but even then he already knew how to make a computer eat out of his hand, and, in fact, he made a computer help him solve a matrix problem that was giving me trouble. Since then he has become an expert on algorithms and polynomial time tests.

372

R. S. Millman

Rich knows about other parts of mathematics, but first and foremost he is a geometer; he studies Riemannian manifolds and has written some high quality geometry texts. This picture was taken at SIU (Southern Illinois), in Carbondale, but he has been at a lot of other places since then, getting monotonically more and more involved in administrative work.

Bjarni Jónsson

Bjarni does algebra (relational structures and lattices) that looks like logic, or is it vice versa? He is a disciple and a collaborator of Tarski's. The picture was taken at Vanderbilt, Bjarni's home territory (if you forget about his origins in Iceland).

373

374

Leopoldo Nachbin

Leopoldo was discovered when he was a bright young student in Brazil by Albert, Stone, and Zygmund, each of whom visited there, and he was imported to Chicago. He has worked in several parts of mathematics (including approximation theory and topology), but his main concern has been the theory of vector-valued holomorphic functions. He has held down two jobs for many years: for the fall semester of every year he is at Rochester and for the rest of the year in Brazil. The picture was taken in Rochester.

375

C. E. Watts

Some of the best mathematicians in the U. S. have spent a year or two of their youth at Chicago as temporary instructors, and that's what Charlie was when I first met him. His work gets him into homology and cohomology and small categories.

376

G. S. Young and W. R. Zame

The last Rochester picture, for now. Gail (left) is a topologist by birth, but, in addition he has been a dedicated mathematical civil servant all his life. Bill's main interest is analytic functions, usually of more than one variable, and he studies topological problems that they raise.

377

Jean Dieudonné

It's hard to think of a part of mathematics that Dieudonné has not written about. He began his mathematical career by thinking about the analysis of polynomials, but he became a Bourbaki convert early on, and one of Bourbaki's chief scribes, and since then, under his own name or under Bourbaki's, he has published masses of material in general topology, topological vector spaces, algebraic geometry, invariant theory, the so-called classical groups, and, just for dessert, a multi-volume text titled *Foundations of modern analysis*.

Bloomington and Britain, 1973 – 1974

378 – 402

378

Gavin Brown and William Moran

Both Gavin (left) and Bill are Britishers who became Australians in the middle of their careers; they are friends and topological group collaborators. I caught them in Aberystwyth, the first stop of my spring jaunt in Britain in 1973.

J. E. Littlewood

None of his colleagues called him by his first name, but, by the same rules that produced that result, not even the most junior fellow at Trinity was supposed to give him his formal title. "Littlewood" was the right form of address for all of us. He was 88 when he hospitably showed me around the college, and his arthritis had nearly crippled him, but he was in good spirits. Mentally he was completely alert, and physically he enjoyed his dinner at the high table, his snuff, and his port. Mathematically he was one of the giant real analysts of the century.

D. G. Northcott

When I first knew Douglas, he was a visitor at Chicago; this time I visited him in Sheffield. He does rings and things, up to and including homological algebra.

380

381

R. V. Kadison and J. R. Ringrose

Dick (right) was a graduate student at Chicago when I was a callow assistant professor there. In class his navy experience showed (he called me Sir), but outside class we were first-name friends. He and John have been collaborating on von Neumann algebras, commuting back and forth between Philadelphia and Newcastle.

382

W. L. Edge

Edge is an Englishman at a Scottish university (Edinburgh); mathematically he has been described as the greatest living 19th century Italian algebraic geometer. He doesn't enjoy the athletic disadvantages of getting on in years; at the height of his powers he thought nothing of getting to a colloquium engagement in Glasgow by walking. (The distance is 45 miles.) Here he is in front of the Mathematical Institute at 20 Chambers Street, the nice old building, which, more is the pity, has been abandoned by the Edinburgh mathematicians in favor of one far away from the center of the city and very modern.

Hans Schneider

Hans, like me, likes matrices of all shapes and sizes, and Hans, like me, is an American of European birth who is a self-appointed Scotsman. Here he is in Edinburgh.

383

E. M. Wright

The last stop of my British jaunt was far North, at Aberdeen, where Wright was Principal at the time (meaning college president, more or less). He was not yet Sir Edward then, but he was famous as a number theorist; his book with Hardy is a classic.

384

385

Constantin Apostol

Ever since 1970 the Wabash Seminar has been meeting almost every month during the school year. In addition to that, in 1973 it met with a bang: Crawfordsville, Indiana, found itself the host of an international collection of functional analysts. Constantin (a member of the talented Romanian mafia) worked in exactly the sorts of things that I am fond of (operators on Hilbert space), and although we had corresponded earlier, this was our first meeting. All but one of the next half dozen pictures were taken at the same conference.

386

M. M. and F. M. Day

Mahlon is one of my oldest mathematical friends, in both senses of the phrase: we met in 1939 at the Institute (in Princeton). He is a Banach spacer, who served for many difficult years as head of the math department at Illinois. Frankie, his wife, has also taught math at Illinois, and it was not a surprise to see them both at the Wabash meeting.

387

M. R. Embry-Wardrop, Pratibha Ghatage, and C. L. Olsen

Three more operator theorists attending the Wabash conference: Mary is at the left, and Cathy in the middle.

388

R. C. James and Sandy Grabiner

Bob (left) knows everything (almost everything?) about Banach spaces; his most famous contribution is an example of a non-reflexive space that is, nevertheless, isometric to its second dual. Sandy's interests are very much along the same lines (operators on Banach spaces, and Banach algebras); in fact it might be fair to call him a disciple of Bob's.

389

J. V. Grabiner

Since she is married to Sandy, here surely is where Judy's picture belongs, even though it is out of chronological order. She is not a mathematician, but as an outstanding historian of mathematics she has often addressed meetings full of people who were, and her scholarship and expository delivery keep filling the house every time. Here she is in San Francisco, in January 1981.

390

Aleksander Pełczyński

Since Banach was a Pole, it was surely appropriate to have a Banach space ambassador from Poland at Wabash.

391

392

Ivan Singer

Ivan is from Romania; he has a gigantic book of two volumes (with a total of more than 1500 pages) on bases in Banach spaces. That is quite different from but not totally unrelated to some of the work of I. M. Singer (#555), and they would both be grateful if we made an effort to keep them straight.

L. D. Berkovitz

Since Lenny was a Chicago student, I have known him for a long time; he was in several of my classes. He was not at the Wabash jamboree; as a control theorist, he had no special interest in it. He is at Purdue, which is not all that far from Bloomington, but scientific intercourse between the two institutions is almost non-existent. It was a rare pleasure to see Lenny, and to be able to snap him during a Bloomington visit.

393

Shmuel Friedland, I. N. Herstein, and Raphael Loewy

Both Raphael (left) and Shmuel are algebraists, from Israel, of more or less the same algebraic persuasion as Yitz (right), whom I have known for centuries. (His first name is Israel, but in this context use of the formal version would probably just be a source of confusion.) Not only is he at Chicago now, but, long long ago, he was a member of the faculty of the curious "College" at the University of Chicago, and we knew each other then. The occasion of the photograph was a get-together at Santa Barbara, in December 1973.

394

J. R. Seberry

The Santa Barbara occasion was where I first met Jennie too. She was Jennifer S. Wallis then, and she has published enough papers under both names (on combinatorics, and, in particular, on Hadamard matrices) to make compiling her bibliography a more than usually hazardous task.

395

Marvin Marcus and Henryk Minc

Marvin and Henryk (another American-European self-appointed Scot) have collaborated so much (mainly on texts and papers on linear algebra) that possibly some people cannot tell them apart; the labelling of the picture might make clear which is which. They are at Santa Barbara, and their picture closes 1973.

396

J. H. Ewing and W. H. Gustafson

John (left) and Bill were my two best friends among the junior faculty at Indiana. John does topology, but he can't help being fascinated by number theory and mixing the two subjects; Bill does groups and things, as well as rings and algebras, but he is knowledgeable about most of modern mathematics. The picture is the first of the few that I took in Bloomington in 1974.

Barry Simon

Another Bloomington picture, but this one is a visitor, not a resident. Barry is a physicist by birth, but every now and then he goes slumming into functional analysis.

397

398

Larry Smith

A topologist, a runner, and a weight lifter, Larry was on the Indiana faculty in 1974; later he became an expatriate, a professor at Göttingen.

399

J. H. B. Kemperman

There was a bit of a statistical wingding at Bloomington in the summer, and Joop was one of the party. He knows about things like probability on groups.

400

Jerzy Neyman

Another member of the party was that irrepressible doyen of statisticians, the incomparable Neyman. He was slightly over 80 when this picture was taken.

401

Emanuel Parzen

Manny was there too; his special expertise is time series analysis.

Jacob Wolfowitz

And Jack closes the list of statistical pictures for now. He was an all-around powerhouse in mathematical statistics; his interests included sequential estimation, queuing theory, and information theory.

402

De Kalb and Vancouver, 1974

403 – 453

Stefan Bergman

Legend has it that Bergman attended Erhard Schmidt's lectures on orthogonal functions and, not knowing German well, thought that the functions that entered were analytic, a happy misstep that led him to discover a new part of mathematics. He never did learn any language well; another part of the legend is that he had a foreign accent even in his native Polish. His mathematical reputation is based, in part, on his kernel function and its applications to conformal mapping. The picture was taken in San Francisco, in January 1974.

403

404

F. P. Greenleaf and G. R. Sell

Another San Francisco picture. Fred (left) is interested in invariant means on topological groups and George in the periodicity properties of solutions of ordinary differential equations.

H. A. Heilbronn

Forty years before this picture was taken Heilbronn laid the foundation of his reputation with his work on asymptotic properties of the class numbers of imaginary quadratic fields.

405

J. C. Scanlon

Jane is my last San Francisco shot in this bunch; some of her work has concerned periodicity properties in non-linear analysis.

406

407

J. R. Blum and C. B. Moler

I caught this pair in Albuquerque. Julius (left) was interested in very pure sounding ergodic theory and, at the same time, in practical sounding statistics. Cleve thinks about numerical analysis in the good old-fashioned sense (what do you have to do with analysis to get numbers out of it?), a subject that the existence of fast computing machines will not put out of business.

408

O. T. O'Meara

Tim hails from South Africa originally, but he has been doing quadratic forms at Notre Dame for a long time, and, more recently, administrative work at increasingly higher levels.

Enrico Bombieri

My 1974 pictures, till this one, hopped around a bit; except for a little P.S. at the end of the year they will now settle down to two locations. The first, and smaller, was an unusually successful and stimulating conference on the problems that were Hilbert's legacy to the generations that followed him; it took place in DeKalb, Illinois, in May. Enrico was one of the chief speakers at that conference. He spoke on (an analogue of) Hilbert's 8th problem, which has to do with the distribution of primes and the Riemann hypothesis. Since sieves and zeta functions are his specialty, he was the right man for the job. Incidentally, I took pictures of all the DeKalb speakers, and thus, as somebody's afterthought, I became the official photographer; my pictures are the ones that appear in the AMS volume that reports the conference.

Herbert Busemann

Herbert is a geometer, and he spoke, in DeKalb, on Hilbert's fourth problem about Desarguesian spaces.

Gina Kolata

Gina was not one of the DeKalb speakers, but her role was, if anything, more important. She is a member of that very rare breed, a mathematical reporter. She is on the editorial staff of *Science* and everyone, expert or tyro, enjoys and learns from her articles.

412

Georg Kreisel

Logic is what Kreisel knows all about, and his subject at DeKalb was Hilbert's second problem, the one about the consistency of arithmetic.

413

414

D. A. Martin

Tony, not Don, seems to be the right thing to call him. He is a set theorist, and his DeKalb subject was Hilbert's first problem, the continuum hypothesis.

J. W. Milnor

Jack is known as a topologist, in recent years as a computer enthusiast, and in DeKalb he spoke on Hilbert's 18th problem, about crystallographic groups, fundamental domains, and sphere packing.

415

H. L. Montgomery

Hugh is a number theorist and, like Bombieri, he too spoke on Hilbert's 8th problem, but he chose to put the emphasis on some of the many still unsolved problems about the distribution of primes.

416

417

David Mumford

Most people think of David as an algebraic geometer; his subject in DeKalb was Hilbert's 15th problem, a rigorous foundation of Schubert's enumerative calculus.

J. L. Selfridge

John was not one of the DeKalb speakers, but, like me, he was there eagerly drinking in the wisdom that was pouring out. As a mathematician he is interested in combinatoric problems, and as a mathematical civil servant he is known for his many years as executive editor of *Mathematical Reviews*.

Olga Taussky

Olga is an algebraist and number theorist who is especially in love with everything that matrices can do; here she is a member of the DeKalb audience. She is sometimes identified as Mrs. John Todd, and at other times as Olga Taussky-Todd—it depends on which directory you try to find her in.

418

419

N. A. Brunswick

The main reason 1974 was a rich source of mathematical photographs is that it was the year of the Vancouver Congress; I had a field day, every day, snapping old friends and new ones. This picture was taken there, in August, as were more than two dozen of the ones that follow, in alphabetical order more or less. Natascha counts as an old friend whom I didn't happen to have shot before. She has many connections with the mathematical world. One of them is that she is a mathematical editor (*Communications on Pure and Applied Mathematics*, the house organ of the Courant Institute), and another is that she is the widow of Artin (#203).

420

E. W. Cheney
Ward is a specialist in approximation theory.

421

Alonzo Church
For almost all of his professional life Church has been one of the world's leaders in mathematical logic, thinking mainly about computability and decidability. "Church's thesis" is what made the vague notion of effectively calculable function respectable by identifying it with the precise concept of general recursive function. He founded the *Journal of Symbolic Logic* and was one of its editors for 43 years.

Alain Connes
Connes' spectacular career started not much before the Vancouver congress. He gave new life to an old subject that some people had been ready to pronounce moribund (von Neumann algebras), and he has been keeping up his profound contributions to it ever since.

422

423

H. S. M. Coxeter

A geometer apparently by birth, his name is associated with many subjects (notably non-Euclidean geometry and polyhedra), and the only thing I once found mysterious about him was why his friends called him Donald. He explained the mystery by signing one of his letters to me with his full name: Harold Scott Mac<u>donald</u> Coxeter.

424

M. D. Davis

What's one of the solvers of Hilbert's 10th problem (about the solvability of diophantine equations), a man interested in such recondite logical mysteries as hierarchies of descriptive set theory, doing at the Courant Institute, a stronghold of useful mathematics? Could the answer have something to do with his knowledgeability about computing machines, Turing and otherwise?

Gerard Debreu

A rare mathematician, he: applying sophisticated theorems about topological vector spaces, he ended up getting a Nobel prize in mathematical economics.

425

426

Pierre Deligne

One of the things that Hilbert and Weil have in common is that Deligne solved Hilbert's 21st problem (about differential equations with prescribed monodromy groups) and Deligne proved Weil's conjectures (about zeta functions of algebraic varieties).

427

L. E. Dubins, Jacob Feldman, and Harold Widom

These are old friends indeed; they were all Chicago students in my day. Harold (left) is a many-sided analyst who has written charming books on Lebesgue theory and on integral equations, and hard papers on the invertibility of Toeplitz matrices. Lester (center) is primarily a probabilist; he is the co-author with Jimmie Savage (#21) of *How to gamble if you must*. Jack likes stochastic processes better than other things, but he has been known to dip an occasional toe into, for instance, the theory of the invariant subspaces of operators.

428

Per Enflo

He burst on the scene with a sudden and unexpected solution of an old problem: there exists, he showed, a separable Banach space that has no basis.

429

J. O. C. Ezeilo and Chike Obi

I had known Jim (right) before the Congress, when he visited Michigan; he does differential equations. Obi does a related branch of analysis, which caused him to publish a long series of papers titled *Analytic theory of nonlinear oscillations*. The last one I noticed bore the ordinal number X.

430

A. H. Fröhlich

Albrecht is a colorful number theorist, mainly algebraic.

431

S. H. Gould

Sydney has a book on variational methods for eigenvalue problems and another on Russian for mathematicians; he worked for many years for the AMS, one of his capacities being editor of *Math Reviews* from 1957 to 1962.

Graham Higman

Graham Higman is a group theorist (he discovered, for instance, a sporadic simple group of his own) who confuses the mathematical world by having interests in common with (and occasionally collaborating with) Don Higman (#224).

432

433

Klaus Peters and Walter Kaufmann-Bühler

Klaus (left) is an active and well known member of the mathematical community whose product, however, is not theorems but books, and the same was true of Walter (till his premature death in 1986). They worked together for Springer for a while, then Klaus joined Birkhäuser, and then Springer bought out Birkhäuser, with the result that it was never easy to tell whether they were collaborators or competitors. This picture was taken during a Springer editorial meeting in Vancouver.

434

E. R. Kolchin

Ellis does analysis algebraically. In his papers on differential algebra words and phrases like "differentiation" and "Galois group" are likely to appear in the same sentence.

435

N. H. Kuiper

Nicolaas' mathematical interests include geometric aspects of analysis; he has, for instance, studied the contractibility of the unitary group on Hilbert space.

436

P. A. Loeb

Peter used to work on potential theory and probability and measure theory, and then he became a convert to non-standard analysis; now he works on potential theory and probability and measure theory from that point of view.

437

E. A. Michael

When I first knew Ernie he was a student at Chicago; some of my colleagues were trying to dissuade him from taking general topology too seriously. He made some penetrating observations about paracompact spaces anyway, and later he became famous for his treatment of selection theorems (which have to do with funcmions that thread their way continuously through a set-valued mess).

438

J. G. Mikusiński

Someone had to make rigorous mathematics out of Heaviside's operational calculus, and Mikusiński did it.

439

Viera Proulx

One of the most fascinating items on the program of the Vancouver Congress was an announcement of the solution of the twin primes conjecture. Viera Proulx presented it, but she was speaking for her father, Frantisek Krňan, who was unable to be present. I didn't understand the talk, and, so far as I know, nothing ever came out of it.

440

Richard Radó and Jacques Tits

Radó (left) is a Hungarian Englishman (professor at Reading), a combinatorialist by conviction; Jacques does groups, and, among other things, is one of the mob that has sporadic groups named after them.

441

E. J. and P. M. Rosenthal

Peter (right) was one of my Ph.D. students and has been an active member of the operator community ever since. Erik is his kid brother; both their affections seem to be evenly split between Hilbert space and political activism. (In comparison with Erik, Peter is a right-wing conservative—or at least that's what Peter says.) On the side, both of them do a lot of writing; one of Erik's recent works is a detective story called *The calculus of murder*.

442

443

Maurice Sion

Maurice's mathematical interests are in measures with values in groups. At the Vancouver Congress he was important for a vital non-mathematical reason: he was the chairman of the local arrangements committee, and, as a result, he was everywhere, doing everything, and doing it very well too.

Stephen Smale

Steve seems to have the Midas touch in many parts of mathematics. His most famous work is the proof of the Poincaré conjecture in spaces of dimension greater than 4; for that he got the Fields medal in 1966.

M. D. Spivak

Mike is a first rate mathematician, but he is known to generations of students for his texts rather than his theorems. He is the author of a seemingly infinite series of volumes titled *A comprehensive introduction to differential geometry.*

444

445

Endre Szemerédi and Pál Vermes

The Erdös-Turán generalization of the van der Waerden theorem about the existence of long arithmetic progressions was an unsolved problem for whose solution Erdös offered a prize of $1000.00; the winner was Szemerédi (left). Vermes's main interests seem to be in very large (infinitely large) matrices.

446

J. L. Taylor

Joe's results are of great interest to me, but I find his methods deep and difficult; he studies Tomita decompositions, Shilov boundaries, and, scariest of all, several-variable spectral theory.

C. A. Truesdell

Clifford is an unusual mixture. He thinks about "real" subjects such as mechanics and thermodynamics, and about their history and their philosophy, but at the same time he is a precise, literate, and highly cultured writer and editor, and the author of many "sermons" (some of which have been collected under the title *An idiot's fugitive essays on science...*). A friendly personal inscription on a reprint that he once sent me says that he never uses the term "applied mathematics" except as a pejorative.

447

448

Karen Uhlenbeck

Perhaps someday I will be remembered as one of Karen Keskulla's classroom teachers (at Michigan). The famous physicist George Uhlenbeck was her father-in-law for a while. She has gone on to become one of the outstanding American mathematicians of her generation, working mainly in what might be called global differential geometry. She finds it natural to use expressions such as Banach manifolds and Yang-Mills fields; when she was colloquium lecturer of the AMS she spoke on mathematical gauge field theory.

Lee Lorch

Lee is a Zygmund kind of trigonometer, but most people don't know that; his main fame for the last fifty years or so has been as a political gadfly of the AMS. His consistency is remarkable: his opinions in the 1980s are not too different from his (then more widely prevailing) views in the 1930s. The picture was taken in New York in October 1974.

449

Dan Voiculescu

We corresponded before we met: he kept solving problems that were too hard for the rest of us (such, for instance, as whether the reducible operators on Hilbert space form a norm dense set). He has left Romania since then, but he is still solving hard problems. And, the alphabet being what it is, this is the last of my pictures from the Vancouver Congress.

450

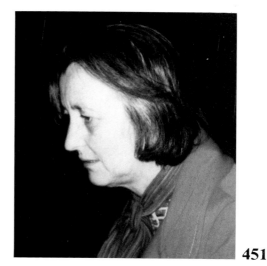

451

C. S. Morawetz

Cathleen is a mathematician in her own right (and a long time member of the Board of Trustees of the AMS) as well as by genetics: her father is J. L. Synge, the well known Irish applied mathematician. Her own main interests are very applied, all about sonic barriers and wave equations. One of her papers is titled *Geometrical optics and the singing of whales.* The picture was taken at the October 1974 New York meeting of what is known as the ECBT (= Executive Committee and Board of Trustees).

452

J. B. Rauch

In November 1974 I was invited to talk to the mathematics club at the University of Michigan. (That's not the colloquium; it's the junior organization whose purpose is to offer expository talks to students). One of the traditions of the club is to permit any member of the audience to give a "three-minute talk" on some topic that currently fascinates him before the main lecture begins. Here Jeffrey (whose main interest is boundary value problems and wave equations) is doing it.

453

D. J. Winter

As long as I was in Ann Arbor I took advantage of the opportunity and shot David; his book *The structure of fields* came out not long before that, and I felt that I had to have him in my collection. When he isn't writing a book he might be caught thinking about non-associative algebras of various kinds, including Lie algebras, of course.

Bloomington to Santa Barbara and back, 1975 – 1978

454 – 506

454

BDF

One of the most spectacular steps forward in operator theory, and in particular in the theory of normal operators on Hilbert space, was taken in 1973. The final result was a profound generalization of the principal axis theorem to infinite-dimensional spaces. The three collaborators who achieved it were L. J. Brown, R. G. Douglas, and P. A. Fillmore; the theorem is commonly referred to as BDF, according to the initial letters of their last names in alphabetical order. When this picture was snapped, in 1975 (in Athens, Georgia), the subjects didn't happen to be standing in alphabetical order (instead they are, from left to right, Peter, Ron, and Larry), but the opportunity was too good to miss.

R. W. Carey and J. D. Pincus

Joel (right) and Richard are frequent collaborators on a part of operator theory (singular integral operators) that is hard enough to be called hard analysis. The photographer at the left is me. The picture was taken (in Athens) by John Ernest, who sent me a copy with the inscription: "Here is the beginning of an induction argument."

455

P. J. Hilton

A professional homologist and homotopist, Peter is a tireless world traveller, who enjoys telling about the time when a colloquium chairman introduced him as an ex-topologist. Here he is in May 1975, on what was then his home territory, in Cleveland.

456

457

R. E. Edwards

Bob is an energetic thinker and writer about functional and harmonic analysis. He is a member of the faculty at the Australian National University in Canberra, but his colleagues don't see him all that much; he prefers to live what some would describe as the life of a recluse. He sticks close to his home, except when he indulges in his hobby of driving much faster than probably anyone should. The picture was taken in Canberra on a slight Australian jaunt that I was able to squeeze into 1975.

458

F. J. Almgren

Fred is a kingpin of geometric measure theory (the name of a difficult branch of hard analysis). The picture is the first of a small bunch that I took at the August 1975 meeting of the AMS at Kalamazoo.

459

R. H. and Mary Bing

R. H. was an outstanding instance of a Texas topologist. He was a disciple of R. L. Moore, probably the most spectacular one. His greatest contributions were to geometric topology, and, in particular, to what might be called the pathology of 3-manifolds. He sounded more Texan than anybody could, and he sometimes had a hard time explaining to people that he was never given a first name or a middle name: he was R. H., no more, no less. (I have even heard the thesis defended that he really was R H–no periods.) He produced scads of Ph.D. students and scads of papers, and took an active part in the necessary work of mathematical organization, having served as president of both the MAA and the AMS. He and Mary were the parents of what I call scads of children (four), but more and more, as the children could be turned loose, Mary accompanied R. H. to meetings. Here they are in Kalamazoo.

Leonard Gillman

Lenny doesn't always have a beard, but I caught him with one. He is the co-author (with Jerison) of *Rings of continuous functions*; he served for many years as treasurer of the MAA, till he had to quit because he was elected president.

460

461

J. R. Isbell and E. E. Moise

John (left) sometimes thinks about uniform spaces and Ed about the triangulation of 3-manifolds, but at Kalamazoo they found something to talk to each other about. Ed was famous as an educator also, in the days of the new math, and as the author of texts that students could learn from or swear at according to their tastes.

462

B. J. Pettis

Billy J. was an abstract analyst at a time when there were very few such people; his name is associated with, for instance, an integral all his own.

463

V. S. Pless

Vera took both algebra and measure theory from me at the University of Chicago and went on to become first a working algebraist (*The continuous transformation ring of biorthogonal bases spaces*) and then a leading coding theorist.

464

Irving Reiner

Irving was an algebraist; his book with Charlie Curtis, *Representation theory of finite groups and associative algebras*, is widely quoted.

465

T. F. Banchoff and J. H. Ewing

Tom does a lot of lecturing, often on spaces of dimension 4 and more, and he does it like a pro—beautifully and with workmanlike attention to all details. Here (standing) he is examining the film he is about to show as part of a 1975 lecture in Bloomington. John was in charge of the colloquium that afternoon.

Eberhard Hopf and P. C. Rosenbloom

Eberhard (right) was a permanent member of the Indiana faculty. His contributions to analysis, both pure and applied, are startling in their extent and their depth: he is the Hopf in Wiener-Hopf operators, he contributed to turbulence theory and to the study of the Navier-Stokes equations, and he proved the ergodicity of the geodesic flow on surfaces of constant negative curvature. Paul was a colloquium visitor to Bloomington in November 1975. He is a student of Tamarkin's, and mathematically he is a man of many parts. He has thought about Post algebras, and published a little book on logic, but much of his work is analytic. He has written about partial differential equations, an infinite-dimensional kind of linear programming, and also the perturbation of the zeros of analytic functions. Somewhere along the line he became interested in elementary education and worked at it full time for many years; he was a national power in many of the decisions and subsequent trends in what mathematics to teach in grade schools and high schools and how to do it.

J. F. Treves

The first name (Jean) is usually kept secret; he is almost always known as François. His works include two books on subjects that are not always studied by the same person: one on topological vector spaces and one on partial differential equations.

467

468

R. G. Newton and C.-N. Yang

Roger (right) is a very mathematical kind of physicist at Indiana who is occasionally chairman of the physics department. When I first knew Nobel laureate Frank Yang he was a graduate student at the University of Chicago and he audited many mathematical courses, including one of mine. Unlike the sterotype bogey-man physicist envisaged by most mathematicians, Frank insists on doing mathematics mathematically; before he calculates with an infinite series he convinces himself that it converges. And don't ask me why Frank is the name he most frequently answers to.

469

Antoni Zygmund

I was proud to be a friend and colleague of Antoni's at Chicago. He is a gentle man (and also a gentleman), and he is often kinder than is good for him; he probably holds the Chicago record for the number of Ph.D. theses written under one person's direction. His English is fluent and excellent, but it sounds more like Warsaw than Chicago. At tea one day, when we were discussing a delicate point of syntax, someone asked him: "Do you still want to polish up your English?" He sounded a bit wistful when he answered: "No, I'd rather English up my Polish." Here he is at a party after his Bloomington colloquium lecture in 1975. The other more or less visible figures are Jan Jaworowski at left (topologist, at Indiana), the back of Alberto Torchinsky's head (complex analyst at Indiana), and Bernie Morrel at right (operator theorist at the Indianapolis branch campus of IU).

Mark Kac

Mark was a probabilist almost by birth whose interests grew to be more and more applied as he grew older. He liked to make jokes, and, for instance, he proudly described himself as the very opposite of an essential singularity: "I am only a simple Pole", he said.

470

471

I. C. Gohberg and H. P. Rosenthal

Israel (left) and I corresponded while he was still in Kishinev, and
we became friends when we first met in Oberwolfach; his work
in operator theory (much of it in collaboration with M. G. Kreĭn)
makes him an important member of the circles I like to move
in. Haskell is a Banach spacer who proves deep theorems about
infinite-dimensional Banach spaces by proving deep theorems about
finite-dimensional ones first.

472

R. L. Wilder

In February 1976 I was invited to Santa Barbara
for an interview, and there met my old friend
Ray, a leading topologist and, as a serious hobby,
a philosopher of mathematics. He and I had
been colleagues at Michigan; when he retired from
there he moved to Santa Barbara, established
connection with the University of California there,
and continued to be happily active. He was 79
when this picture was taken.

473

Karol Borsuk and B. E. Rhoades

Borsuk (left) was a leading member of the Polish school of topology interested mainly in homotopy theory. Here he is visiting Bloomington, where Billy, whose main interest is summability, was a colleague of mine.

474

M. C. Gemignani

Michael's chief mathematical interests are set-theoretic topology and combinatorics, but he doesn't stop there. When I knew him he was also active as an Episcopal priest, as mathematics chairman of the Indianapolis branch of Indiana University, and as a law student who was subsequently admitted to the bar. Later he went more and more into administrative work; last I heard he was a dean at Ball State, and, on the side, he conducts a column in the magazine *Abacus* on computers and the law.

P. E. Conner

Pierre is a topologist, a frequent collaborator of Ed Floyd's (#135). I caught him on a quickie visit to his home territory (Baton Rouge), and I found it interesting to learn that his middle name is Euclid.

475

Masamichi Takesaki

I did move to Santa Barbara in 1976, and one of the first things I did was to set up "Wabash West" (more or less in imitation of the successful Wabash seminar). A famous inter-university seminar of the same sort has been run for many years by the universities at Edinburgh and Newcastle under the name NBFAS (North British Functional Analysis Seminar, pronounced N - B - Fas); it was natural to call the new one SCFAS (for Southern California, pronounced S - C - Fas). It met, for a while, at Cal State Northridge, and that was where I caught Takesaki, a von Neumann algebra expert.

476

477

J. T. Schwartz

The German word for black is not schwartz, it is schwarz. The one with the inequality was German and spelled his name right; the currently famous ones (Laurent and, as here, Jack) use an Eastern European misspelling. Jack's first fame came from being co-author (with Nelson Dunford) of an encyclopedic treatise on linear operators. He has done many things since then (including von Neumann algebras); one of his domains of expertise nowadays is computer theory (and practice). Both this picture and the next one were taken at an AMS Council meeting in New York.

478

L. A. Steen

If you want an example of a separable and metrizable Hausdorff space that is paracompact but not sequentially compact and is totally disconnected but not extremally disconnected, all you have to do is to look on the right page of Lynn's book (*Counterexamples in topology*) that he wrote with Art Seebach. Other than that he has been very active in the affairs of the MAA, up to and including serving a term as president.

479

A. T. Bharucha-Reid

When I first met Al, in the early 1950s, he was studying mathematical biology at the University of Chicago. This picture was taken in August 1976 but I can't remember where. In any event he grew into a mathematician, active in probability and statistics; he became dean of the graduate school at Wayne State, and a few years later he died suddenly and prematurely, soon after he was elected a member of the Council of the AMS.

480

Anil Nerode

When I first knew Anil he was a graduate student at Chicago (where I taught him rings and things) and his name was Chowdhury. One concept that fascinated him for quite a time was that of an "isol" (which is a special kind of equivalence class of sets of natural numbers). His interest has always been in foundational subjects.

481

Lars Gårding and H. F. Weinberger

Another picture in England: Lars (#79) and Hans
are PDE conspirators. Hans (right) and I became
friends when we worked happily together on the
editorial board of the *Bulletin of the AMS*.

T. W. Gamelin

Ted's part of soft analysis (function algebras) is near enough
mine to interest me and far
enough to be difficult. Although
he is a Californian, I caught
him in Newcastle.

482

483

484

E. T. Copson

He is the author of a widely used book on complex function theory and was the grand old man at the 1976 meeting of the St. Andrews colloquium, where this picture was taken.

Arthur Erdélyi

Arthur was Hungarian by birth, but in the profession he was known as a Californian (for the years he spent in Pasadena as editor of the work Harry Bateman left behind) and a Scotsman (for the years he spent at Edinburgh). His specialty was special functions.

485

R. S. Varga

Another Hungarian, sort of. Dick was born in America, but he lives in the Cleveland area, and Cleveland is the second largest Hungarian city in the world. Dick speaks Hungarian (better than I do) and seems to feel himself a part of the Hungarian culture. Mathematically he is a numerical analyst. The picture was taken in Santa Barbara. All my 1977 pictures were taken in California, but my records for that year are not in perfect shape, and (with apologies for incomplete information) I must confess that in many cases I cannot be sure exactly where I took them.

486

Y. N. Moschovakis

Yiannis (is that Greek for John?) is at UCLA, a logician and set theorist, and in his case I know that I snapped him on his home base.

487

T. T. Frankel and S. E. Warschawski

Ted (left) could be called a topological geometer (manifolds) and Steve a complex analyst (conformal mapping), and I caught them during a Southern California swing.

488

M. W. Hirsch

Moe, on the other hand, belongs to my Northern swing; his home base is Berkeley. He is an expert on hard topology, such as immersions of smooth manifolds, and I want some of the credit; I gave him an *A* in an introductory topology course (set theoretic, to be sure) at the University of Chicago.

R. J. Milgram

I knew Jimmy before he was born, by knowing his father, Arthur Milgram, whose greatest fame is hyphenated (the Lax–Milgram theorem). Jim's work in topology has established him as a first class mathematician in his own right.

489

490

S. L. Greitzer and M. S. Klamkin

Sam (left) almost single-handedly caused the U. S. to become interested in mathematical olympiads and to participate in the international ones; Murray is a dedicated problem solver and Sam's heir as chief executive officer of the olympiads.

491

G. L. Alexanderson and Juris Hartmanis

Jerry (right) is a combinatorialist, a busy editor, and even busier administrator. He knows the subtitles of all the Gilbert and Sullivan operettas. Juris knows about automata theory, Turing machines, computational complexity, and all like that. The picture was taken while the three of us were serving as a review committee to examine the mathematical activities of San Diego State University.

492

R. F. Arens

Richard started life as a "topological algebraist" whose name is attached to more than one result about topological vector spaces. The older he got, the more physical he got, writing about dynamical systems, and quantum mechanics.

493

Ky Fan and W. A. J. Luxemburg

It's hard to find a part of mathematics that Ky (right, pronounced key) hasn't worked in, but the concept of convexity might be the guiding thread through it all; I was pleased and proud to have him as a colleague at Santa Barbara. Wim too has worked on different kinds of problems. He collaborated with Zaanen (#564) on a long series of papers about Banach function spaces, but he is perhaps best known for his advocacy and expositions of non-standard analysis.

J. E. Marsden

I think of Jerry as an applied mathematician (Hamiltonian mechanics, momentum operators), but he has also written about topology (net convergence), and is known for his texts: many students learned calculus from them.

494

W. P. Thurston

Bill's visualization of phenomena of low dimensions (such as 2 and 3, but sometimes 4 or even 5) is what has made that branch of topology a major industry nowadays; here he is, in Santa Barbara in 1978, already well started on his spectacular career.

J. C. Kiefer

Jack might have been called a statistician by professional affiliation, but he was a mathematician in his techniques and insights; he worked in queuing theory, order statistics, and multivariable optimality.

Leonidas Alaoglu

His name is Turkish, his principal cultural heritage was Greek, and he spoke English like someone who was brought up in Canada. Leon's name is attached to one of the basic theorems of functional analysis (about the weak* compactness of unit balls in conjugate spaces), but after a running start he spent much of the rest of his life as a spectator and an applier of mathematics, working in industry. The picture was taken in 1978 in Los Angeles.

498

G. M. Bergman

George does algebra (semigroups, groups, rings, modules, fields, and algebras) and he enjoys making algebra out of everything. The picture was taken in Berkeley, his home territory.

499

Robin Hartshorne

Robin is a geometer, one of the ones who removes the mysteries by turning the subject into algebra—witness his books explaining projective geometry and algebraic geometry.

R. C. Kirby

Rob (whose first name is Robion) took measure theory from me at Chicago in 1959, but it didn't seem to impress him. He is one of the solvers of the Hauptvermutung, and won the Veblen prize in 1971.

500

501

R. M. and J. B. Robinson

Raphael was one of the first people involved in the theory of primitive recursive functions; he has a genius for making everything he touches clean and sharp and comprehensible in a finite context. He was one of Julia's early teachers, and from that beginning he became her husband and she went on to become one of the solvers of Hilbert's 10th problem, and, incidentally, president of the AMS.

502

Laurent Schwartz

Nothing in mathematics comes out of nothing, and, in particular, various kinds of generalized derivatives had been studied by analysts before Laurent Schwartz came along. I think it is fair to say, nevertheless, that he by himself started a whole new part of mathematics when he offered his discovery of distributions to the world. One of his first papers on the subject had the impressive title (I am translating) *Generalization of the notions of function, differentiation, and Fourier transform, and mathematical and physical applications.* Here he is on a visit to Berkeley in 1978.

S. J. Friedlander

Susan is an applied mathematician (fluid dynamics), who works slightly south of the Loop (at the Chicago branch of the University of Illinois); this picture was taken in 1978. Its presence here justifies me, I think, in placing the next picture out of chronological order.

503

504

W. G. Dwyer and E. M. Friedlander

Bill (left) is a very algebraic topologist; he indulges, for instance, in K-theory, and when I visited Notre Dame in April 1986 he was chairman of his department. Eric does mathematics very similar to Bill's, and very different from Susan's (whose husband he is), and he does it at Northwestern, way far north of Chicago's Loop.

W. R. G. Haken

He and Ken Appel have offered a solution of the four-color problem, a solution consisting of a lot of thought and a lot of computation. I am sorry that I don't have a picture of Ken to put along with this one (which, by the way, was taken in August 1978).

505

S. C. Kleene

When I was trying to learn logic Steve's book was the one I found most honest and most helpful. Most people pronounce his name in two syllables, almost as if it were spelled Klee-nee.

The Poincaré conference,
Budapest, and between,
1979 – 1982

507 – 554

507

R. M. Smullyan

The 1979 winter meeting of the AMS was originally set at some totally inappropriate place for a winter meeting (I seem to remember Milwaukee), and at the last minute it was moved to the South. That's why many of us suddenly found ourselves in Biloxi, where this picture and the two that follow it were taken. Ray used to earn his living as a professional magician, he is a concert caliber piano player, and he has been fascinated all his life by self-reference. The name of one of his books is *What is the name of this book?*, and the title of another is *This book needs no title*. Surprise: his specialty is the Gödel incompleteness theorem.

508

A. I. Thaler

Al used to be an algebraist, as I remember, but for many years now he has had to give all his energies to the NSF, whose money he tries to give away as wisely and as stingily as he can.

509

G. W. Whitehead

George followed a well-established topological tradition by labeling his book on homotopy as volume 1; the last I heard I was advised not to hold my breath till volume 2 comes out. His current hobby is genealogy.

510

David Finkelstein and A. M. Gleason

In May of 1979 there was a conference in New Orleans whose main focus was physics, or, rather, the physical applications of certain operator-theoretic concepts. Laboring under the misapprehension that just because I know something about shift operators I must therefore know what they are good for, the organizers invited me to attend (but, fortunately, not to speak). I met David there (left) who does research in "topological physics" (words like "spin" and "kinks" enter), and I re-met Andy, whom, of course, I have known for a long time. He has many claims to fame; one of them is his contribution to the solution of Hilbert's fifth problem (about Lie groups).

511

Robert Hermann

Bob used to be mainly a differential geometer, but that fact sometimes gets lost among his other spectacularly productive activities. He writes a lot of mathematics and, acting as a publishing company (Math Sci Press), he publishes some of it himself. Between times he is a vociferous disagreer about many aspects of the way the mathematical world is run. In outlets such as the *Notices* and *The Mathematical Intelligencer* he argues emotionally in favor of more support for engineering and scientific mathematics. He deplores the structure that permits the existence of two mathematical cultures (pure and applied) and permits the elitist pures to be rigidly in charge of the status quo.

512

A. M. Jaffe

Arthur is very much a member of the mathematical commmunity, but although his work uses phrases such as selfadjoint operators, it is really about bosons and quantum field theories—by profession he is really a physicist.

513

E. M. Stein

Eli is a student of Zygmund's; I remember torturing him on at least one examination when he was at Chicago. His work is on the hard analysis part of harmonic analysis: he interpolates between Banach spaces and he finds strange representations of semisimple Lie groups. Here he is spending a week as distinguished visitor in Bloomington.

D. R. Hofstadter

Doug's father, Robert Hofstadter, is a Nobel prize winning physicist. Doug himself jumped from an unknown student to an international celebrity when his book *Gödel, Escher, Bach* appeared. I caught him when he was a member of the faculty of Bloomington (in computer science); from there he moved to Michigan (in many departments, including, the way I heard it, psychology).

514

Gabriel Stolzenberg

Gabriel is an honest-to-goodness mathematician (analytic varieties), and at the same time (although he would probably resent my making any distinction) an ardent believer in and expounder of Errett Bishop's constructivism. Here he is on a Bloomington visit.

515

Underwood Dudley

Woody is at DePauw (although this picture was taken during a visit to the Wabash seminar), and he is an editor's dream (as well as, frequently, an editor himself). He is a problem solver, a reliable and tough referee, and, incidentally, an expert on mathematical cranks—angle trisectors and the like. A few years ago he made a lot of enemies, and friends, by publishing a note titled *Mathematics: who needs it?*

516

517

René Thom

The mathematical world as a whole associates Thom's name with catastrophe theory, which made headline news in the 1970s, but topologists had known him long before that as one of the early developers of cobordism. During his Bloomington visit in 1979 he gave a public lecture on catastrophes and a colloquium talk on differentiable manifolds.

Garrett Birkhoff

Young people tend to confuse Garrett with his father, G. D. Birkhoff, classical analysis powerhouse at Harvard in the first half of the century. Garrett's first claim to fame was his book on lattice theory, and his subsequent work in other fields has a hard time replacing that claim. According to a possibly apocryphal story, when early in Garrett's career G. D. was told that Garrett was almost as good a mathematician as G. D. himself, the old man said "I always knew he was good, but I didn't know he was *that* good!"

518

519

Michael Aschbacher

Michael was one of the solvers of the classification problem for simple groups; the picture was taken in Bloomington in February 1980.

520

Victor Kac

He does representation theory; graded Lie algebras are in the picture.

J. F. Adams

This is the first of a sequence of pictures taken at the Poincaré conference in Bloomington in April 1980. Frank is a topologist (homotopy groups, vector fields on spheres, spectral sequences, cohomology operations) who is also a rock climber. If you dare him to, he'll walk completely around your living room (with the aid of the fireplace, bookcases, window frames and anything else he can touch and temporarily hang on to) without his feet ever touching the floor.

521

522

Errett Bishop

Errett was without a doubt my best student at Chicago. His thesis was on operator theory, but he branched out and became an important figure in other branches of analysis (several complex variables, function algebras), and he is the founder of the mathematical religion called constructivism. In the copy of his book that he gave me he inscribed "To Paul, in hopes that you don't find it too outrageous, Errett."

F. E. Browder

Felix is the oldest of the Browder brothers (#338). He has worked on elliptic PDE's and he was one of the developers of George Minty's ideas about monotone operators.

523

524

R. M. and T. V. Fossum

It is not easy for an outsider to tell the brothers Fossum apart mathematically. Tim (left) does rings and groups and Bob does groups and rings. The search committee looking for someone to replace Everett Pitcher as Secretary of the AMS has suggested that Bob be the only candidate for the job.

525

Harry Fürstenberg

In some directories Harry's name is given as Hillel, and when he explained it all to me I got the idea that it depended on which country he was in at the time. He works on topological dynamics, which is a variety of ergodic theory, and he makes it work in surprising ways; he gave, for instance, an ergodic theory proof of Szemerédi's theorem (#445) about the existence of long arithmetic progressions in sparse sequences.

Jean Leray

A name to conjure with, a name known to mathematicians of all kinds—Leray is associated with concepts as far apart as spectral sequences and hyperbolic PDE's. I was introduced to him three different times once when he was in Chicago, and he said a polite "enchanté" each time, but had no idea that there had been earlier times. I was upset then, but I am more sympathetic now; after a certain age one just doesn't remember everything or everybody.

A. L. Liulevicius

It's all right to call him Arunas, but he isn't at all sure that he wants to be called "Arnie". Here he is a distinguished topologist, attending the Poincaré conference. When I first met him (as a student at Chicago), I was supposed to be teaching him advanced calculus, including the sort of topological subtleties that that awkward subject is for most of us the first introduction to.

J. P. May

Peter is another algebraic topologist; the last time I ran into him he was chairman of the math department at Chicago.

D. S. Ornstein

Don is Kaplansky's Ph.D. student, but, I am proud to say, I am the one who taught him ergodic theory, and he went on from there in a blaze of glory.

529

Roger Penrose

Another one about whom it is hard to say whether he is in physics or math; he thinks about general relativity both as mathematics and as cosmology. In view of Poincaré's own mixed feelings, Roger was just the right kind of person to have at the conference.

530

531

D. P. Sullivan

Dennis knew about the *Hauptvermutung* before most people, and in 1971 he got the Veblen prize for what he found out.

Daniel Zelinsky

Dan was a Ph.D. student of Albert's (algebra, of course), and we met when I went to Chicago (in 1946). Soon afterward he accepted a job at Northwestern, up the road a piece, and he has been there ever since. I don't know why, but there wasn't much back and forth visiting between the Chicago department and the one at Northwestern; I was more likely to run into Dan at a random AMS meeting in Kansas. This picture of him was taken on the occasion of Ralph Boas's retirement party in May 1980.

532

533

L. O. Collatz and Vlastimil Pták

Collatz (left) is sometimes called an applied mathematician (who writes, for instance, about eigenvalue problems with technical applications), but he knows about pure functional analysis (and can tie it up with numerical methods), and is even credited with being one of the discoverers and early workers on the celebrated number theory problem identified by the expression $3x + 1$. Pták is near the other end of the diameter; his functional analysis is on topological vector spaces and he studies, for instance, the closed graph theorem in barreled spaces. The picture was taken in Budapest on the occasion of a gigantic international conference in honor of the 100th anniversary of the birthdays of both Fejér and F. Riesz.

Tsuyoshi Andô

On the way back from Budapest I attended an Oberwolfach Tagung, and met Andô, whose name I had known and respected for a long time; he is one of the leading figures in the operator community.

534

535

R. K. Guy

Richard is a dedicated problem solver and problem spreader. Proof: see his book on unsolved problems in number theory and his long-time and continuing editorship of the department of unsolved problems in the *Monthly*. As a part of his editorial work he has published several biennial reports on the subsequent status of the problems (that is, their partial or complete solutions, if any), which aficionados have been finding of great interest and value. This picture, and the next three, were taken at the AMS meeting in San Francisco, in January 1981.

Raoul Hailpern

Raoul has been the power behind the throne of the *Monthly* for one editor after another longer than he likes to think about. I couldn't have done my *Monthly* job without his dedicated, fussy, and always correct work, and I am sure that every other editor that he worked with would say the same about him. In recent years it has become a tradition for all the associate editors of the *Monthly* to have a dinner meeting once or twice a year, at the national meetings of the Association, and that's the occasion on which I caught Raoul in San Francisco.

536

M. E. and Walter Rudin

What do the Rudins talk about at home?
They have four children, Mary Ellen, a
student of R. L. Moore, thinks about hard
set theory and topology, and Walter, while
not writing an infinite number of books,
thinks about measures in groups.

537

538

D. W. Schattschneider

Doris thinks and writes about
geometry, is an expert and ex-
perienced editor, and is a wife
and a mother. It's not for me
to say which of these activities
she is best at.

539

George Piranian

George is a complex analyst, he speaks Armenian, he regularly attends the beer seminars of Ann Arbor's speakers of that absolutely impossible dialect called Swiss German, and he is remembered by many as the editor of the *Michigan Mathematical Journal* who enforced the rules of correct English with an iron fist in an iron glove. I caught him on his home ground, in Ann Arbor.

540

Gaisi Takeuti

Some people think that as mathematicians logicians are too narrow, but that rumor doesn't seem to have reached Takeuti. He is interested not only in logic, and set theory, and ordinal numbers, but also in the operational calculus and in real honest to goodness operator theory, of the kind that the Wabash seminar frequently discusses. Here he is, addressing the Wabash seminar in September 1981.

541

E. F. Beckenbach and R. L. Finney

Ed (right) has a famous book on inequalities (with Bellman) and was for a long time chairman of the publications committee of the MAA. The picture was taken in Cincinnati in January 1982, at a meeting of that committee. Ross thinks about the subject that used to be called combinatorial topology—is that exactly the same as algebraic topology? His father is the well-known composer of the same name.

D. T. Finkbeiner and A. C. Tucker

Another shot at the same committee meeting. Dan (right) is perhaps best known for his text on matrices; Alan's mathematical interest is in combinatorics, and incidentally in computers and their applications. He is the son of Al Tucker (the Princeton topologist and combinatorialist, #130) and the stepson of Ed Beckenbach (#541), from whom, a little later, he inherited the chairmanship of the committee.

542

543

J. W. Addison

John is a logician two ways: in his own right and as a son-in-law of Alonzo Church (#421). In between times he is, off and on, chairman of the math department at Berkeley. The picture was taken at an MAA meeting in Davis, California, in February 1982.

S. W. Golomb

Sol knows all about combinatorics, including games of all kinds; here he is talking about games to the MAA meeting in Davis.

544

P. L. Renz

Another attendant at the Davis meeting that year, Peter, as a mathematician, has been known to think about topology in Banach manifolds. Nowadays he has to do that in his spare time, whenever being Associate Director of the MAA allows him to.

545

546

G. H. Golub

A lot of people when they think of computer science face west and bow low in the direction of Gene Golub. I caught him when I was about ready to give a colloquium talk at Stanford.

Samuel Karlin

Is he a convex mathematician, an applied statistician, a game theorist, an economist, or a biologist—or is Sam some of all those things ?

547

H. L. Royden

Halsey (which some people dare contract to Hal) does complex functions when he isn't writing one of the most widely used real function theory books, or deaning or chairmanning (at Stanford).

548

R. W. Hamming

The biggest problem in information theory seems to be to conceal the information so as to make it easy to find. This is called coding, and Dick is famous, among other things, for the Hamming code. Here he is, at home, at the Naval Postgraduate School in Monterey.

M. H. Stone

Marshall is one of the grand old men of American mathematics. His contributions include the representation theorem for unitary groups of operators, the representation theorem for Boolean algebras, the Stone–Čech compactification theorem, and the Stone–Weierstrass theorem. This picture was taken in Bloomington in March 1982, about a month before his 79th birthday.

C. I. Foias and B. Sz-Nagy

Ciprian (right) is from Romania and Béla from the next door part of Hungary. They are a famous pair of collaborators, working mainly on operator theory in Hilbert space. Béla can speak some Romanian, but the language they use between them is either French or English, depending, apparently, on where they are. Here they are at a meeting of the Wabash seminar in March 1982.

Wabash

Speaking, as I often have, of the Wabash seminar, here is a typical shot (taken in April 1982). Unfortunately I do not know the names of all the people shown, but I'll list the ones I do recognize. At the center foreground is Bill Swift, our principal host; I don't know who is half hidden behind him on the left. The others, starting from the top left, are Marc Raphael, Jerry Kaminker, Owen Burkinshaw, Sandy Grabiner, Carl Cowen (just to the right of Bill Swift), a nameless listener (to the right and behind Carl), and Bob Olin.

553

Steve Armentrout

It was a pleasure to attend ECBT meetings of the AMS with Steve (he served on the Board of Trustees as Associate Treasurer): neither he nor I believed in the so-called continental breakfasts that the early morning session began with, and we usually met over cereal, bacon, and eggs beforehand. Mathematically Steve has had a long-standing friendly feud about the Poincaré conjecture: he thinks it's false and has felt himself close to a counterexample once or twice, whereas Everett Pitcher thinks it's true and has thought he almost had a proof once or twice. Since Everett doesn't object to continental breakfasts quite as much as Steve does, they usually conduct their feud over lunch and dinner. The locale this time is Ann Arbor, in May 1982.

554

S. M. Ulam

Stan's early work was on set theory (measurable cardinals) and topology (with Borsuk). He was a problem lover, closely associated with the famous Polish *Scottish Book.* During and after the war he went on to help invent the hydrogen bomb (in Los Alamos), and on the side he (and von Neumann) proposed what has come to be called the Monte Carlo method for approximating the solutions of otherwise unsolvable problems.

Mainly meetings,
1982 – 1986

555 – 606

**M. F. Atiyah and
I. M. Singer**

Both Michael (Sir Michael to
you, on the left) and Izzy (Yitz
to some old friends) are known
for many major accomplishments, but together they are a
hyphenated theorem, the Atiyah-
Singer index theorem. I caught
them together on a visit to
Berkeley in February 1983.

555

556

P. A. Griffiths

He knows about algebraic varieties and the intri-
cacies of administration; when last seen he was
Provost at Duke. Here he is in Berkeley.

557

F. W. Gehring

Fred's main mathematical interest is in quasiconformal mappings, and at the drop of a hat he'll rush off to Finland to work with the quasiconformalists there. He finds time also for being chairman at Michigan (more than once), for being editor of several Springer book series, and for being a member of the Board of Trustees of the AMS. Here he is at a Springer editorial meeting in San Francisco.

558

C. C. Moore

Cal's specialty is unitary representations of things, and, aside from that, he finds many things in common with Fred Gehring: he too has been chairman (at Berkeley), as well as dean, and he too used to be a Springer editor, and on the AMS Board of Trustees. When, however, he became a vice president at Berkeley, he threw in the towel on most of those activities.

559

Jan Mycielski

Jan's early work was in set theory, but he has thought about games and topology. He was clearly influenced by the Polish logical atmosphere, and is familiar with concepts like the axiom of determinacy. Here he is on a Bloomington visit in April 1983.

560

W. M. Schmidt

Another Bloomington visitor at about the same time, his specialty is analytic number theory, and, in particular, transcendental numbers.

561

John Dyer-Bennet

John loves mathematics; if he weren't a real pro, and if the French word didn't have pejorative connotations, he should be called a genuine amateur. He is a dedicated and deservedly popular teacher. Here he is on his home base, at Carleton (in Minnesota). Some non-mathematicians, old enough to remember a few decades back, might remember his name as that of a popular folk singer, but that's not John—it's his brother Richard.

P. J. Sally

Paul is a harmonic analyst, involved with unitary representations, Fourier transforms, and the like, and he too is a manifold administrator. He has been chairman at Chicago and has served on the Board of Trustees of the AMS.

562

563

H. S. Shapiro

Harold has appeared here before (#243) but there he was almost invisible. Here he is in Oberwolfach, in August 1983. His main field of interest is approximation theory.

A. C. Zaanen

Adriaan and I overlap in many interests, including measure theory and functional analysis. At the time this picture was taken (in August 1983) we were overlapping in Oberwolfach.

564

A. J. Hoffman

Alan does real mathematics, like convexity and matrices and other such linear-like things, but he does it for IBM. Here he is at the AMS meeting in Albany in August 1983.

565

D. P. Roselle and K. A. Ross

David (left) does combinatorics and Ken harmonic analysis (witness the gigantic book on the subject written with Ed Hewitt). David was secretary of the Association, till he became Provost at VPI, when Ken became secretary in his place.

566

Marshall Hall

Marshall is an algebraist, and, in particular, a finite groupie (his simple group is a small one, of order 604,800), but he is also the author of one of the standard bibles of combinatorial theory. Here he is in Evanston, in November 1983.

567

J. A. Thorpe

John does differential geometry, except when he gives NSF money away. Here he is on his normal home territory in Stony Brook in November 1983.

568

569

Melvin Hochster

Mel is a first-rate algebraist, and, rumor has it, when several universities recognized his merits and made him offers, he decided to decline them all and stay at Michigan, provided that he would not have to be chairman. He is, nevertheless, very effective at administrative work, and, in particular, has been an effective member of the Executive Committee of the AMS. That's what he is doing here, in Providence, in November 1983.

Israel Halperin

Iz works in operator theory; he has been an ardent admirer of von Neumann all his professional life. He is a Canadian and a political activist on what is for many people the unpopular side, and, as a result, he has been in trouble more than once, about, for instance, being allowed to enter the U.S. Here, on his home territory in Toronto, in November 1983, he seems harmless and mellow, which is how I myself have always found him.

570

**R. J. Blattner and
M. S. Montgomery**

I knew Bob back in Chicago as a student; he does group representations. Susan is a number theorist, and according to some state laws she should really be called Mrs. Blattner. The picture was taken at the Louisville meeting of the AMS in January 1984.

571

572

L. A. Caffarelli

The folder he is carrying off the stage is the Bôcher prize that he was just awarded. He works on things like Navier-Stokes equations, jet flows, and the dam problem; he has frequently collaborated with Avner Friedman (#353).

573

M. G. Crandall and J. E. Osborn

John (left) and Michael are attending a meeting of the Council in Louisville, but it sure looked as if they were talking mathematics, not Council business. What lends more plausibility to the suspicion is that Michael studies differential operators and John studies eigenvalue problems for unbounded operators.

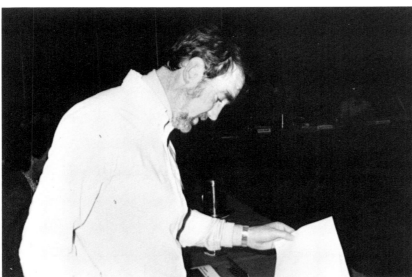

574

R. P. Langlands

Bob is one of the leaders of modern mathematics, working on hard stuff such as automorphic forms and their zeta functions. His strength is not only in proving theorems but in asking questions; one of the central aspects of unitary representation theory is the Langlands conjecture about how to get some of them.

B. C. Mazur

I don't think Barry would be offended if he were described as a topologist, possibly with the modifier "differential". He has worked on the Schönflies problem (which is related to the Jordan curve theorem in higher dimensions), has thought about imbeddings of spheres, and is one of the solvers of the Hauptvermutung. At the Louisville meeting of the AMS in 1984 he was colloquium lecturer; the title of his lectures was *On the arithmetic of curves.*

575

576

R. B. Melrose

This picture was taken at the Louisville Council meeting; its subject is an applied mathematician who writes on things like "propagation of singularities along gliding rays".

J. E. Taylor

Jean, another Council shot, works on minimal surfaces; she has been known to talk about soap bubbles, of course, and crystals too.

577

578

R. A. Askey

I caught Dick during a Bloomington visit in March 1984. His specialty is special functions, such as ultraspherical polynomials and Jacobi polynomials; a part of his work was involved in de Branges' solution of the Bieberbach conjecture.

Gerd Faltings

The spectacular mathematical explosion in 1983 was Faltings' solution of the Mordell conjecture. Many mathematicians who are not number theorists were innocent about the Mordell conjecture, but nobody was ignorant about one of the corollaries of the result: it follows that while the infamous Fermat conjecture could still be false, the number of independent counterexamples is finite. (The word "independent" intends to prevent us from regarding (x, y, z) and (cx, cy, cz) as different.)

579

580

Louis de Branges and D. E. Sarason

Louis (right) has worked on several parts of analysis, but his spectacular and never-to-be-forgotten contribution is the solution of the Bieberbach conjecture about the Taylor coefficients of univalent functions. Here he is chatting with Don at a meeting of the Wabash seminar in the spring of 1984. Don is an operator theorist and complex function theorist, and, I am proud to say, one of my Ph.D. students.

581

Sheldon Axler, P. B. Gorkin, D. E. Sarason, and P. R. Halmos

Speaking of my Ph.D. students, I couldn't resist the temptation of inserting this picture here. It was taken at a conference in Lancaster (England) in 1984, and it represents four mathematical generations. I am at the right, next to me is Don, my student, next to him is Sheldon, his Ph.D. student, and next to Sheldon is Pam, who is, of course, Sheldon's Ph.D. student.

582

J. W. Helton

Bill can talk on equal terms with both very pure mathematicians and very applied engineers; one of his papers, for instance, is titled *Non-euclidean functional analysis and electronics*. The picture was taken at the Lancaster conference.

Shunhua Sun

One of the advantages of international conferences (such as the one in Lancaster) is the chance it gives us to meet colleagues from far away. Shunhua is a case in point; I was in touch with him about his solution of some non-trivial operator problems, long before we were able to get together. (I have put the name in the customary Western order, with given name first and family name last.)

583

584

Alberto Torchinsky

Alberto was a colleague of mine in Indiana, and I caught him in Bloomington (after the Lancaster conference). He appeared in these pages before (#469) but almost invisibly. He is fond of analytic functions of at least one complex variable, but he has also been known to do some deaning (of Latino affairs). His picture here ends the ones taken in 1984.

Constance Reid

Constance is often invited to talk to groups of mathematicians, and that's what she was doing in February, 1985, when this picture was taken in Menlo Park, California. The reason she is invited is that she is a witty speaker and that she knows more about mathematicians than any other non-mathematician. She comes by her knowledge partly through study and research (of which she had to do a tremendous lot to produce her books on Hilbert and Courant and Neyman) and partly through inheritance, if that's the word: she is the sister of Julia Robinson.

585

586

T. M. Apostol

The quantity of Tom's books is not maximal among prolific mathematical authors, but their quality is uniformly high; he writes calculus for smart undergraduates and analytic number theory for smart grown-ups.

R. E. Block

Dick is still another ex-Chicago student. Now he is an established algebraist who was one of the invited lecturers at the Laramie meeting of the AMS in 1985; he spoke on simple Lie algebras of prime characteristic.

587

588

B. H. Gross

This picture of Benedict Gross, known as Dick, was taken in 1985 in Providence. I was attending the March ECBT meeting, and so was Dick's wife, Jill Mesirov, an important official of the AMS at the time. On that occasion Dick was merely a spouse who lucked out — his presence earned him a free meal. In 1986 he got a MacArthur fellowship and in 1987 the Cole prize in number theory for his work on imaginary quadratic fields.

Stephen Simons

Stephen was the mathematics chairman at Santa Barbara who hired me in 1976. When he is not an administrator he is a functional analyst, but here, in June 1985, he is administering the conference honoring Ky Fan (#493) on the occasion of Ky's retirement.

589

590

W. L. Duren

Bill likes mathematics and mathematicians, and vice versa. When I first met him, in the 1950's, he was chairman at Tulane, and he has played many other important roles in the mathematical world since then. He was, for example, president of the MAA for a term, and, for another example, he is the father of Peter Duren. The picture was taken at the Laramie meeting of the AMS in August 1985.

591

F. R. K. Chung and R. L. Graham

Both Ron and Fan are mathematicians, both work in combinatorics, both work for the telephone company (Bell), and both are married. To each other. Ron is known especially for his interest in and contributions to Ramsey theory, and he plays an active role (for instance as a member of the Board of Trustees) in the affairs of the AMS. He has also been president of the International Jugglers Association. Here they are in Laramie.

592

Ernst Snapper

Another Laramie picture, this time of a well-known group theorist who knows about cohomology and who is fascinated by the philosophy of mathematics as well. Ernst spent years at Indiana, but before my time.

David Gale
David is a mathematician, a game theorist, an economist; here he is in Berkeley, on his home grounds.

593

594

V. F. R. Jones
Another Berkeley picture, in September 1985. Vaughan surprised the mathematical world by seeing a connection between the topology of knots and the analysis of von Neumann algebras.

595

Lenore Blum

Lenore has published joint papers (on inductive inference) with her husband, Manuel, and she believes in being active all the time. One of her many activities has been the study (and sometimes even cure?) of the disease known as math anxiety.

Gerhard Ringel

Four colors may be enough for maps on the sphere, but for orientable surfaces of higher genus (spheres with holes) more colors are needed. For a sphere with one hole (a torus) the magic number is seven; as the number of holes becomes 2, 3, 4, 5, and 6, the number of colors that might have to be used becomes 8, 9, 10, 11, and 11. These results are contained in the old Heawood formula, and Ringel was one of the people who proved (with Ted Youngs, #20) that the formula worked. He is at Santa Cruz, and that's where this picture was taken in December 1985.

596

597

B. A. Reznick and R. P. Stanley

Bruce (left) and Richard are both problem lovers, and I caught them here, in Santa Clara, making up problems for one of the Putnam exams of the future. Richard does combinatorics. Bruce is good at answering questions that other people ask him; in between he thinks about algebra, and number theory, and even, in unguarded moments, Banach spaces. And that brings to a close the penultimate year, 1985, of this album.

598

H. M. Bacon and Hans Samelson

Harold (left) has been at Stanford for what may seem like centuries and is universally loved and respected for being a great teacher. Hans is one of my best friends even if he is a topologist, and he has been at Stanford for what seems like only one century. Here they both are at Davis, California, at a meeting of the MAA, in February 1986.

Alice and Max Zorn

Max is the mathematician in this family, he of the lemma, and I was lucky to catch them in a happy mood on a visit to Bloomington in March 1986. He was three months less than 80 years old when the picture was taken. The last I heard he still shows up at his office every day, attends colloquia and seminars, and asks seemingly innocent but usually sharp and sometimes embarrassingly sharp questions.

C. M. Byrne and J. H. Conway

Catriona is a mathematician by training and a Springer editor by profession. Here she is at Hull (England) at the April 1985 meeting of the BMC with the John Conway who is not to be confused with John Conway (#265). This John Conway can be challenged to solve other people's problems (and, for instance, he too has a simple group of his own to his credit), but he is especially famous for thinking up striking and original problems of his own. He loves games and makes up new ones; often he wears shoes.

600

601

C. P. Rourke

Colin was one of the featured speakers at the Hull BMC he tried to make us understand his offered solution of the Poincaré conjecture. He is a serious and respected member of the topological community, and the audience, though somewhat bewildered, received the message in a friendly spirit; the experts tell me, however, that they are not yet totally convinced.

602

Anita and Solomon Feferman

Sol is a logician, a disciple of Tarski's, and a historian of logic; he is, in particular, an expert on Gödel. Sometimes, as here in May 1986, he is chairman of the mathematics department at Stanford. Anita, in case you're wondering, is his wife.

603

Yitzhak Katznelson and P. W. Jones

Yitz (or Izzy, in any case the one on the left) is a harmonic analyst, who seems to alternate between Stanford and Jerusalem. Peter does harmonic measures, Hilbert transforms, and the like, and when this picture was taken he was a visitor at Stanford.

604

P. W. Diaconis

Persi (pronounced Percy) is a magician, a probabilist, and incidentally a stimulating lecturer. He sometimes says that he is interested in solving the mathematical problems of "the real world," by which he means studying the statistical problems of ESP research and applying the theory of representations of symmetric groups to card shuffling. I was lucky to catch him at Stanford; when the Harvard offer came, he didn't refuse it.

605

John McCarthy

There is a small set of people each of whom is sometimes referred to as the father of artificial intelligence, and, in particular, the inventor of the term; John is a member of that small set.

606

T. A. Lehrer

Known to almost every mathematician (of a certain age) and to many others, Tom Lehrer is witty, musically talented, irreverent, and fascinated by mathematics and mathematicians. The picture was taken in San Jose in June, 1986—and that's about as cheerful a note to end this album on as any could be.

Index

Index

Index

Index

Index

Truesdell, C. A., 447
Tucker, A. C., 542
Tucker, A. W., 130
Tukey, J. W., 133
Turán, P., 147
Tutte, W. T., 218
Twin primes, 439

U

Uhlenbeck, K., 448
Ulam, S. M., 554

V

van der Waerden, B. L., 228
Varga, R. S., 485
Vermes, P., 445
Voiculescu, D., 449

W

Wabash, 552
Walker, G. L., 333, 334
Walker, R. J., 258
Wallace, A. D., 166

Wallace, A. H., 261
Wallen, L. J., 222
Walsh, J. L., 143
Warner, S. L., 6
Warschawski, S. E., 487
Washnitzer, G., 188
Watts, C. E., 375
Wehausen, J. V., 76
Weil, A., 18, 236
Weinberger, H. F., 482
Weiss, G. L., 286
Wells, R. O., 341
Wermer, J., 28
Weyl, F. J., 320
Whitehead, G. W., 61, 509
Whitehead, J. H. C., 55
Whitehead, K. B., 61
Whyburn, G. T., 72
Widom, H., 427
Wielandt, H., 533
Wilansky, A., 268
Wilder, R. L., 472
Wilf, H. S., 186
Wilks, S. S., 66
Williams, J. P., 216
Winter, D. J., 453
Wirsing, E., 224

Wold, H. O. A., 126
Wolf, J. A., 274
Wolfowitz, J., 402
Wright, E. M., 384

Y

Yang, C.-T., 187
Yang, C.-N., 468
Yosida, K., 51
Young, G. S., 376
Young, L. C., 281
Youngs, J. W. T., 20

Z

Zaanen, A. C., 564
Zame, W. R., 376
Zariski, O., 279
Zassenhaus, H. J., 108
Zeeman, E. C., 60
Zelinsky, D., 532
Ziemer, W. P., 331
Zorn, A., 599
Zorn, M., 599
Zygmund, A., 237, 469